MEMORIES IN MOMENTS

Over 600 timeless ideas for celebrating life's special occasions

By Susan Stone
Illustrated by Roxane Murphy Smith

MARALLY PUBLISHING

"A Celebration of Ideas"

MARALLY PUBLISHING
Suite B
P.O. Box 1426
Mukilteo, WA 98275

MEMORIES IN MOMENTS
Copyright ©1998 by Susan Stone
First Edition
Second Printing

Cover design and illustrations by Roxane Murphy Smith

Design and pre-press: Jeanie James, Freelance Graphics

Library of Congress Catalog Card Number: 98-91624

ISBN: 0-9664733-0-2

Printed in the United States of America.

DEDICATION

This book is dedicated to:

My wonderful mom and dad,
who gave me a childhood filled with fun and magical traditions . . .

My amazing husband,
for his never-ending support and encouragement . . .

and

My two lovely daughters,
who give me such a sense of pride and happiness . . .

You are my inspiration, and I love you all dearly.

A special thank you
to the following experts for their creative ideas!

Jack Albrecht	Sherry Hoonan
Lois Albrecht	Lisa Jacobson
Karen Berasi	Jeanie James
Sue Foster	Roxane Murphy Smith
Leslie Gilchrist	Maureen O'Neal
Laurel Granger	Diana Paradis
Barbara Hagstrom	Daria Roche
Lori Halsen	Melody Scherting
Kim Haub	Jackie Slosson
Kathy Henderson	Carol Wester
Sheryl Hirsch	Pat Vegsund

The Teachers at Endeavour Elementary, Mukilteo, WA

INTRODUCTION

MEMORIES IN MOMENTS is designed to simplify your life by providing an abundance of fun, time-saving ideas for celebrating life's special occasions.

Each idea is accompanied by a symbol for easy reference:

 Baking and menu suggestions

 Decorating

 Fun and games

 Gifts

 Simple gestures

Many ideas have been modified in each chapter to illustrate how easy it is to simply change one activity, decoration, or dessert to fit your occasion.

Record your own ideas and special memories in the note pages provided at the end of each section. That way, not only will you have an invaluable resource, but a family keepsake as well.

Enjoy the moments with the special people in your life!

TABLE OF CONTENTS

WINTER

WINTER TRADITIONS

⌂ Create a magical winter entrance to your home with "ice luminaries." If the weather outside is freezing cold, it's the perfect time to decorate your porch for entertaining. Ice luminaries are easy to make, but they require a little pre-planning. Save your half-gallon milk cartons. Fill each halfway with water and either set the cartons outside in freezing weather, or put them in your freezer. It will take about eight hours to freeze a sturdy outside shell of ice (the center will not be completely frozen). Peel away the carton. Use a spoon to break the ice on top, and pour out the water—you will have a hollowed out block of ice. Set this on your porch or along your walkway with a small candle inside.

⌂ Incorporate your children's outgrown winter accessories and toys such as ice skates or a small wooden sled into your winter decorating. Hang your children's smallest mittens on garland or tie them onto a wreath.

⌣ Keep a variety of cocoa mixes on hand. If you like to make your hot chocolate from scratch, try substituting white chocolate or chocolate-mint flavored chocolate for semi-sweet.

♡ Winter is the time to pull out all the candles, throws and quilts, and cuddle with loved ones by the fire.

Snowmen

Have fun playing in the snow with your kids, making snow angels, having a snowball fight, and, of course, building your one-of-a-kind snowman, snow lady or snow creature!

Here are just a few suggestions to get you thinking. Potential accessories could be . . .

Things found in nature:
- Evergreen or holly sprigs
- Holly berries or any other winter berry
- Pine cones
- Small rocks
- Twigs (great for antlers, arms, tails or wild hair)

Items around your house:
- Clothing including accessories
- Clothespins
- Colorful small lids from plastic milk jugs or yogurt containers
- Metal coat hangers (untwist and bend into a variety of shapes).
- Sand pails or plastic food storage containers for "molds"
- A variety of spray bottles filled with different colors of food coloring and water
- Small toys or other props
- Star garland or any other trim

Edible decorations:
- Fruits or vegetables
- Nuts
- Sunflower seeds in the shell
- Popped popcorn

Let your imagination run wild!
You could create:

Rudolph:
- Twigs for antlers
- A small red ball, a red milk or yogurt lid or a small red apple for the nose
- Rocks for eyes

Vegetarian Snow Lady:
- Broccoli hair
- Carrot nose (what else!)
- Black olives for eyes
- Red pepper cut into lips
- Celery stalks (complete with leaves) for arms
- Mushroom buttons
- Potato shoes

Nature's Friend Snowman:
- Pine cones spread with peanut butter and birdseed for the hair
- A corn cob for the nose
- Sunflower seeds in the shell to form a smile
- A necklace made from a string of popped popcorn

Mermaid:
- Sculpt the body and a long fish tail. Use spray bottles of colored water to embellish her long flowing hair, facial features, bathing suit (or use a real bathing suit top or shells) and the colorful scales of her fish tail.

Angel:
- Use coat hangers twisted into triangular shapes for wings and a small halo. You could add star garland, or weave an evergreen sprig around the wire. If you want to get elaborate, you could even form her snow arms around a snow bowl and insert a small candle.

Decorate windows with your children's handmade paper snowflakes. Or decorate your windowsills with faux snow. With a hand mixer, combine 4 cups of soap flakes (not detergent) with 2 cups of hot water and beat until thickened.

Make snowman desserts. Stack two scoops of vanilla ice cream on each plate. Set out bowls of colorful, edible decorations. Use strips of fruit leather or gummy worms for scarves, pretzels or crispy chow mein noodles for arms, chocolate chips or raisins for eyes, and pieces of orange gumdrops or candy corn for the nose. You could even sprinkle on shredded coconut "snow."

Bring in a bowl of clean, fresh snow, drizzle maple syrup, juice or pop over the top and enjoy!

For a fun winter indoor game for younger children, have a "snowball" hunt. Hide cotton balls and give each child a knit hat to collect them in.

Plant sweet peas on Presidents' Day weekend, and enjoy beautiful and fragrant bouquets all during the summer.

Help your kids warm up after a day of playing in the snow. Put dry clothes in the dryer for about 10 minutes to warm up before changing.

Display pictures on your refrigerator of your family enjoying winter activities—past and present.

Make a few snowballs and save them in a plastic bag in your freezer. This summer bring them out to make real snow cones.

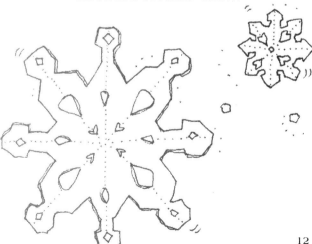

12

NOTES

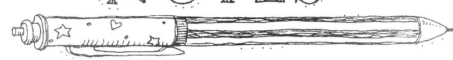

NOTES

Christmas

♡ Take a break, pour yourself a hot cup of tea or coffee, and remember what made the holidays so memorable for you when you were younger. Your children are not going to remember every gift they received, but they will remember the special family traditions that make your celebrations unique. Make a promise this year to limit the holiday activities, savor this time with your family, and remember the true meaning of Christmas.

Walk through your neighborhood to admire the Christmas lights, especially magical after a new fallen snow. Or fill your car with friends, play holiday music, and take a drive to see the lights. Come home to cookies and cocoa.

Keep copies of your children's letters to Santa. Encourage them to write one every year, no matter how old they are! If they are too young to write, have them draw a picture. Buy a special Christmas album to display the letters and drawings. Another idea is to buy one Christmas journal for them to write their letters in each year. On Christmas Eve leave this out so that Santa can read their entry.

Who doesn't enjoy receiving Christmas mail? Turn your Christmas stockings into personal holiday mailboxes in the house. Tuck a candy cane in each. When the cane is hooked on the outside, it means mail is in! During the month, tuck in envelopes with special messages. Encourage your children to return the mail so that everyone will be able to enjoy their stockings before Christmas morning. (See "Baskets," pages 62 & 63, for some stocking stuffer ideas.)

Make wreath cupcakes. Frost cupcakes with white frosting. Dye coconut with green food coloring and, while frosting is still soft, sprinkle the coconut on the edges to form a wreath. Use cinnamon dots or other small red candies for the berries, and pipe on a colorful frosting bow.

Steep your home in the fragrances of Christmas. Purchase scented candles and potpourri scents in spiced apple cider, cinnamon, cranberry, pine, sugar cookie or vanilla.

If someone you love is going to be away from home or just needs a little help getting through the holidays, make their Christmas as special as it can be. Wrap up 24 small holiday gifts and a special one for the 25th. Gifts can be anything small like holiday ornaments, cookie mix, a cassette or CD, holiday napkins, etc. Number them from 1 to 25, and wrap each item a little differently. Include a note: "Starting with number one, open one gift each night just before dinner!" Put all of the gifts in one big box and schedule delivery for the day after Thanksgiving.

Take a photograph on Christmas of your kids with their new toys in front of the tree. It's fun to look back on these and reminisce . . . "I remember when I got that!"

Keep a basket filled with holiday books that only come out at this time of year. Add a new one to your collection each Christmas and put a message and the year in each one. On Christmas Eve, when the pajamas are on, teeth brushed, and cookies set out for Santa, this might be a nice gift for the family to share. Curl up in front of the Christmas tree and enjoy the moment.

Top cakes and cupcakes with decorated cookies in holiday shapes.

Record a family Christmas message on your telephone answering machine.

To cut down time when wrapping multiple gifts for the same person, make a wrapping paper or ribbon "key." Take a piece of paper and write each person's name. Alongside each name, put a small piece of holiday wrapping paper or a piece of ribbon used just for their gifts. It's an easy way to identify gifts without writing all the tags!

Make cinnamon applesauce ornaments. They're fun to create and make great gifts. Use them also to embellish a ribbon on a package or a homemade baked item. Tie them onto a garland or wreath. Here's the recipe:

1 cup ground cinnamon
4 Tablespoons allspice or a mixture of ground cloves and nutmeg
1 cup applesauce
2 Tablespoons white glue

Mix together until you reach a stiff consistency. Add more applesauce if needed. Dust a cutting board with cinnamon and roll the dough to a half-inch thickness. Using cookie cutters or patterns, cut into holiday shapes. If creating hanging ornaments, poke a hole in each with a drinking straw before baking. Place onto a cinnamon-dusted cookie sheet and bake at 350 degrees approximately 25 minutes (time may vary, depending on the size of the pieces).
    Note: These are non-edible.

Give theme gifts to the special families on your gift list that encourage togetherness. Some examples:

• Camping: Fill a duffel bag with a map of the stars (you could wrap around a string of star garland), travel games, ingredients to make s'mores, a flashlight or a small lantern, a book of ghost stories (if age appropriate), and a compass.

• Cookie: Fill a basket, plate or mixing bowl with a cookie cookbook, cookie cutters, a pot holder or oven mitt, some pastry bags and decorating tips, and a variety of sprinkles. Wrap with cellophane and tie with a pretty ribbon and a cookie cutter. If using a Christmas theme, give this gift early in December.

• Games: Fill a big box or basket with a board game, a dice game, a deck of playing cards with a "how to" book on card games, and an outdoor game.

• Ice cream basket: Put in some old-fashioned ice cream sundae cups, long-handled spoons, fun napkins, and assorted jars of toppings and sprinkles. If you really want to get elaborate, package this inside of a large ice cream maker.

• Movies: Fill a large personalized popcorn bowl with assorted videos or Christmas classics, popcorn, and a shaker of seasonings or a cookbook on making flavored popcorn.

• Winter: Buy a big plastic inner tube and fill the middle with a fluffy sheet of imitation "snow." Put in cocoa mixes, mugs and a variety of bright ear muffs, mittens, and hats.

Think about what the lucky family would enjoy early in the year. Many items may be only available seasonally.

What do you buy for the special teachers in your children's lives? Here are a few ideas from the teachers themselves:

- A card from the parents with a positive letter telling that they appreciated the teacher's efforts and inter-actions with their child. So often teachers only hear negative feedback.

- A group present from the students of a gift certificate pertaining to their teacher's personal interest, hobby or collection. Or give a gift certificate to a bookstore. Do not set a dollar amount for students' donations, but let each child or family contribute what they feel comfortable giving. This way everyone can share the enjoyment of presenting the gift to the teacher.

- Christmas ornaments that include the child's name and the date on the back.

- A school-theme accessory relating to their teacher's expertise. For example: A music teacher might enjoy a tie or scarf decorated with instruments. Give a librarian a whimsical pin in the shape of a book.

- A gift for the classroom that would be a decorative or educational addition. Some ideas: an age-appropriate hardback book that could be enjoyed year after year (write the class or name of the giver on the inside). Make or purchase personalized book-ends, a chalkboard eraser, a pencil holder cup, or a hand-painted frame to hold the current class photograph.

- A small poinsettia or mini-ature Christmas tree, or a small plant to be enjoyed all year.

- Note pads or removable adhesive notes to be used for the many notes sent home to parents during the school year.

- A yearly or ongoing photo album or scrapbook. Organize a few parent volunteers to take pictures. Have each of the children write a memory of what they enjoyed most about their year or teacher.

Least favorite gifts: Anything with an apple motif, mugs, candy, knick-knacks, after-shave or perfume.

Start a tradition of a "Secret Santa" month with older kids. Everyone in the family draws a name and throughout the month each person puts a little treat in their chosen person's stocking. This could be as simple as a note, a HERSHEY'S KISSES® chocolate, a small gift, or a coupon redeemable for a chore or special favor.

For an extravagant outing, spend the night at a downtown hotel. Enjoy the holiday decorations and treat your family to a "Santa Breakfast" at one of the hotels, or see a holiday show. After a day of Christmas shopping, come back to your room and have room service send up a pot of hot chocolate.

Put a small artificial Christmas tree with lights in each of the children's bedrooms. Let them choose their own decorating theme.

Buy or make a Christmas quilt for each child to be used only during the cold winter months.

If your child's birthday falls on or right around Christmas time, decorate a small "birthday tree." Hang strands of brightly colored curling ribbon, small party favors and balloons. Use a party hat for a tree topper.

Have a family slumber party one weekend with sleeping bags in front of the Christmas tree.

Give a present to your feathered friends. Decorate an outside tree by hanging pine cones that are spread with peanut butter and dipped in birdseed.

Keep out a Christmas photo album which you add to each year. Decorate your refrigerator with pictures and special greeting cards from past holidays.

Give a gift of new pajamas on Christmas Eve. No one wants to be in ratty old pajamas for those morning Christmas pictures!

♡ When your kids visit their grandparents' home at Christmas, ask grandma and grandpa to share with your children the memories or stories of special ornaments and decorations that they used when you were young. Children love to hear about the meaningful things you enjoyed as a child.

🥣 Before serving your holiday dessert, decorate the dessert plates. Write names or a holiday message with a squeeze bottle of chocolate or raspberry syrup.

🎁 Buy each of your children a Christmas music box on their first Christmas (or start this tradition now). Put the date on the music boxes, and let the children enjoy their new heirloom by placing the music boxes on bedside tables.

♡ Start a Christmas morning tradition. Have a cup of hot chocolate poured from a Christmas teapot. Take a moment to enjoy the sight of the decorated tree with the beautiful packages beneath it and the filled stockings.

🕊 Take a drive to the mountains to a tree farm to find the perfect tree. Make a day of it. Pack a lunch, complete with a thermos of hot chocolate or spiced cider.

🎁 Make a family project out of designing your Christmas card. Capture a family Christmas or winter tradition. What does your family enjoy most? Going to cut down your tree? Baking Christmas cookies? Sledding? Ice skating? Skiing? When you are having fun as a family, you're sure to get a great picture. Think ahead and bring your camera. One original design is to make a family collage. Take pictures of your family's special moments during the year. Pick the favorites and make photocopies. You might want to include a holiday letter telling about your year.

Key Idea

Recreate Santa's snowy footsteps. Moisten the bottom of a boot with water, dip it in baking soda, and make footprints on the hearth.

Buy a special plate that reads "Cookies for Santa" and also include your children's names and the year purchased. You might also want a personalized bowl for "Carrots for Rudolph." Incorporate these into your holiday decorating.

Enjoy a German tradition: Hide a pickle ornament on your tree on Christmas Eve among your other hanging ornaments. The next morning, the first person to find the pickle receives a small gift.

Bake reindeer cookies. Make sugar or gingerbread cookies and cut into small heart shapes with a cookie cutter. Frost with tan frosting and use chocolate chips for the eyes, and a cinnamon dot candy for the nose. Use either broken pieces of small twist pretzels or crispy chow mein noodles for the antlers.

When wrapping a child's gift, tuck a candy cane into the ribbon.

Use a small living Christmas tree one year, instead of buying a pre-cut one. Then plant it in your yard for an evergreen memory.

Start a holiday collection and get the whole family involved. For example, you might collect antique children's wind-up toys or Christmas books, Santa figures, snowmen or winter villages. Make a family project out of hunting for additions at antique shops, garage sales, on vacations, or when you are just shopping around town. Also, look for accessories to display with your collection. Use your imagination and enjoy your excursions!

CARROTS FOR RUDOLPH !

The "Tray Game" is fun to play at a Christmas party. On a tray, place a variety of Christmas items. For example: a candy cane or other wrapped holiday candy, a candle, a Christmas card, a Christmas cookie, a Christmas light bulb, a holiday napkin, an ornament hook, a pine cone, a Christmas postage stamp, a small piece of Christmas ribbon, a small snip from your Christmas tree, a walnut, a small piece of Christmas wrapping paper and anything else you can think of. Bring out the tray and let everyone look at it for about one minute. Then remove the tray. Give everyone a piece of paper and a pencil and set the timer for three (or more) minutes. See who can write down the most items from memory.

A variation of this game: Put additional items on the tray that are not related to Christmas. For example, have everyone list only the non-Christmas items, or only the items that are red. This game can be modified for any holiday.

Take a family picture with Santa from the time your children are babies until they leave home. Display them in a special place.

Start a tradition of serving a special family recipe of cinnamon rolls, a sweet roll in the shape of a wreath, a breakfast bread, or any other favorite recipe on Christmas morning. When your children marry, pass on the recipe along with a holiday plate or pan.

Hang jingle bells on gift bags, shoelaces and pets' collars. Hang sleigh bells on your front door.

Make an ongoing family Christmas video. Include footage of the preparations as well as the actual day. Be sure to video tape the decorations and as many candid moments as you can. Play a different holiday song in the background each year.

Cut down on your baking time and enjoy a night out with friends by having a Christmas cookie exchange. Invite over five friends and have each of them bake six dozen cookies. Everyone keeps a dozen and gives each friend one dozen. If you want to exchange recipes as well, have everyone bring five recipe cards with the cookie recipe written down.

Give new life to favorite outgrown Christmas pajamas or sweatshirts. Make each child a special holiday pillow out of them.

Resist the urge to "correct" the way the kids decorate the tree, even if all the ornaments are on the bottom half! You will have great pictures and an instant "growth chart." If you wish, buy an additional tree to decorate in another room.

Remember those who are less fortunate. You and your family might collect pennies and other loose change in a jar all year. At Christmas time, choose a few names from a giving tree and buy toys for these children, or blankets and toiletries for adults and children at a local shelter. Another thought: Purchase teddy bears to be used by police or fire departments in emergencies involving children. Your options are limitless, and the lesson to your children will be invaluable.

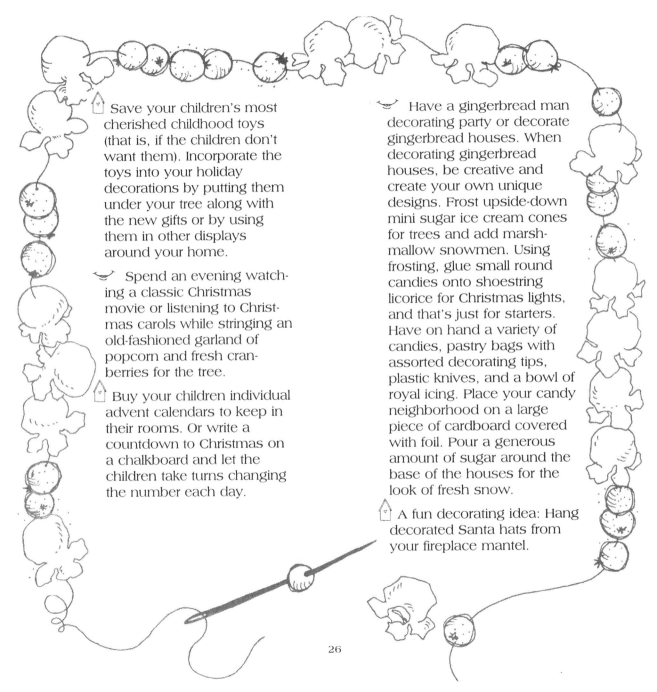

Save your children's most cherished childhood toys (that is, if the children don't want them). Incorporate the toys into your holiday decorations by putting them under your tree along with the new gifts or by using them in other displays around your home.

Spend an evening watching a classic Christmas movie or listening to Christmas carols while stringing an old-fashioned garland of popcorn and fresh cranberries for the tree.

Buy your children individual advent calendars to keep in their rooms. Or write a countdown to Christmas on a chalkboard and let the children take turns changing the number each day.

Have a gingerbread man decorating party or decorate gingerbread houses. When decorating gingerbread houses, be creative and create your own unique designs. Frost upside-down mini sugar ice cream cones for trees and add marsh-mallow snowmen. Using frosting, glue small round candies onto shoestring licorice for Christmas lights, and that's just for starters. Have on hand a variety of candies, pastry bags with assorted decorating tips, plastic knives, and a bowl of royal icing. Place your candy neighborhood on a large piece of cardboard covered with foil. Pour a generous amount of sugar around the base of the houses for the look of fresh snow.

A fun decorating idea: Hang decorated Santa hats from your fireplace mantel.

NOTES

NOTES

Happy New Year!

Spend New Year's Eve with your family playing games. Set up several game tables with a different game at each one. Set a timer to signal the end of each game. When the timer goes off, whoever is ahead wins! Then everyone switches to a new table. This is one way to keep everyone awake until midnight. Prizes for the winners might be small inexpensive gifts or lottery scratch tickets. If you have small children, buy a few extra as consolation prizes.

If you prefer that younger children not stay up until midnight, set an alarm clock to an earlier hour and enjoy your "midnight" celebration a little early.

Sprinkle your tablecloth with confetti and small curls of brightly colored curling ribbon. For a fun centerpiece, fill a basket with a variety of party hats and noisemakers. Tie on a note that reads "Happy New Year!"

Have everyone write several predictions for the New Year. Don't tell anyone what you wrote. Put the papers in a manila envelope with next year's date written on the outside and seal it. Bring this out next year and see how many came true.

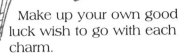

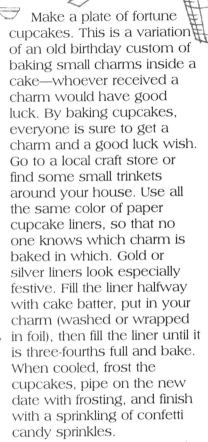

Make a plate of fortune cupcakes. This is a variation of an old birthday custom of baking small charms inside a cake—whoever received a charm would have good luck. By baking cupcakes, everyone is sure to get a charm and a good luck wish. Go to a local craft store or find some small trinkets around your house. Use all the same color of paper cupcake liners, so that no one knows which charm is baked in which. Gold or silver liners look especially festive. Fill the liner halfway with cake batter, put in your charm (washed or wrapped in foil), then fill the liner until it is three-fourths full and bake. When cooled, frost the cupcakes, pipe on the new date with frosting, and finish with a sprinkling of confetti candy sprinkles.

Note: This is not appropriate for very young children. Make sure everyone finds the charm first to avoid choking.

Make up your own good luck wish to go with each charm.

- One dice: You will win a contest or lottery.
- Star charm: You will be famous one day.
- Car charm: You will travel to a faraway place.
- Light bulb charm: You will be a famous inventor.
- Penny wrapped in foil: You will have great wealth.
- A shoe charm: You will become a great athlete or win a race.

. . .The possibilities are endless!

For a fun party favor, make New Year's Eve eyeglasses. You might want to make this an activity for the evening by offering different colors of papers, glue, glitter, colored feathers, and whatever else you can find around the house. Make a stencil with the new date and trace onto a piece of heavy, shiny paper. Cut out eye holes from the circles within the numbers. Cut out two additional side pieces to go over your ears (paper fasteners will keep the ends in place). Have everyone wear the glasses for a great New Year's Eve picture!

Transform clear plastic champagne glasses into instant New Year's Eve glasses. Stick on gold stars, or write out the year with number stickers. Wrap gold curling ribbon around the base, fill with sparkling cider, and toast the New Year. Or buy special toasting glasses for your family and give duplicates to other family members who will not be with you. At midnight everyone can make a toast and think of their loved ones.

Take time to reminisce. During the year fill a small decorated box with special mementos, theater stubs, programs, photos, awards, notes with funny moments written down, napkins from special places, or items that have special meaning. Have the kids write down the year's funniest time, best accomplishment, and so on, and put them in the box. Each year bring these out on New Year's Eve.

NOTES

Famous Couples Game

Mickey & Mini Mouse
Romeo & Juliette
Beauty an the Beast
Batman & Robin
Raggedy Ann & Andy
Fred and Welma Flinstone
Barny and Betty Rubble
Lady and the Tramp
Adam & Eve
Santa & Mrs. Clause
Tarzan & Jane
Brad Pitt & Jennifer Aniston
Barbie & Ken

Make conversation-heart cupcakes to resemble conversation-heart candy. Frost the cupcakes with white frosting. Create a solid heart design in the middle of each, using a variety of pastel frostings. With dark pink frosting, pipe on a message like "KISS ME," "SMILE," or "TRUE LOVE," and outline the heart.

Save materials throughout the year: ribbon scraps, stickers, plastic gems, designs cut from cards, quotes, etc. Set up a valentine decorating station complete with glue and an assortment of paper and doilies. Send special cards to grandparents, friends, or family members who don't regularly benefit from the joy of children's artwork.

Throw a Valentine's Day party. Have the guests wear something red or pink. Plan a game where guests have to figure out clues and find the objects. Some examples: Find a couple of cards all decked out (the king and queen of hearts playing cards). Find a city in Colorado, the land of love (Loveland, Colorado)—have a map or atlas on hand. Unscramble OKECOI TURTCE (cookie cutter – a heart-shaped one) . . . just a few ideas to get you started!

U. R. NICE

STICKERS

TRUE LOVE

Decorate your refrigerator with your kids' handmade valentines from past years and from other special people in your life.

Surprise your child at school on Valentine's Day with lunch from a favorite restaurant. If you prefer, pack a special lunch. Decorate the lunch bag with heart stickers, rubber stamps, or a funny drawing or saying. Inside, put valentine stickers on anything from an apple to a wrapped sandwich.

Take your Valentine's Day party on the road for a surprise getaway. Check into a hotel, go swimming, order room service or pack a picnic dinner, play games, watch movies and have fun!

Serve heart-shaped pizza for dinner. Spell out "I LOVE YOU" with the toppings.

Leave funny "love notes" all over the house. On a pair of high-heeled shoes, "I'm head over heels in love with you"; on a jar of peanuts "I'm nuts for you"; on the cheese or a cheese sandwich "I know it's cheesy, but you're the greatest"; on a lamp, "You light up my life." Be creative! You could even make a game out of it by putting names on the notes. The first one to find all of his or her messages gets a prize.

Make special Valentine's Day drinks or desserts. Cut maraschino cherries in half and then cut into heart shapes. Put on top of hot fudge sundaes. Or make classic "Shirley Temples" (7 UP® and maraschino cherry juice) or "Roy Rogers" (cola and maraschino cherry juice). Top with heart-shaped cherries.

Order some heart-shaped bagels from your local bagel shop and fill with pink-tinted cream cheese.

For a fun surprise, tuck valentines everywhere, especially in unexpected places. Place next to pillows, in drawers, shoes, pockets, backpacks, notebooks, even inside the cereal box!

Make Valentine's day cookie "lollipops." Cut out two heart-shaped cookies. Before baking, stack two, insert a popsicle stick in between and smooth the sides. When cooled, decorate the cookies with frosting and pipe on polka dots or a special message. Wrap in cellophane and tie with a pretty ribbon for gift giving.

Give your child a special gift that is something you both can share. It might be a storybook, a game, a gift certificate for an outing, or a tea set.

Play HEART bingo with conversation-heart candy for game markers.

Make heart-shaped pan-cakes, waffles or toast for breakfast. Cut with a heart-shaped large cookie cutter or cut a "V" shape out of the top of a round pancake or waffle to form a heart. Serve with strawberry or raspberry syrup or jam and lots of whipped cream.

Punch out designs with a heart-shaped hole punch from a variety of pink, red and white construction or textured papers. Sprinkle them on your tablecloth or in a valentine envelope.

For a fun classroom or children's party, hold a Valentine's Day relay race. Form into two teams. The first person in line passes a red balloon over his head to the person behind. That person passes the balloon between his legs to the next person until it is passed over-under-over to the end of the line. The last person takes the balloon to the front of the line and the game continues until the original player is at the head of the line again.

HAPPY VALENTINES DAY

Key Idea

Leave a trail of HERSHEY'S KISSES® chocolates from your child's bed to a special place where a surprise awaits.

Fill clear lamp bases with conversation hearts, seasonal M&M's® brand chocolate candy, or other wrapped valentine candy.

Tie a valentine mylar balloon (or heart-shaped one on which you've written a message) to your child's bed for a great morning surprise.

Dip red licorice sticks in melted white chocolate and sprinkle with red and pink sprinkles. Use heart-shaped ones if you can find them. Package in a small cellophane bag decorated with a Valentine's Day design or set on the table in a pretty glass.

Play a game. How many words can you make out of the word VALENTINE? (ant, eel, it, lint, nail, nine, tail, tale, tan, teal, ten, tie, tile, tin, valentine, vat and veal . . . to name a few).

Fill vases with red tulips; fill baskets with red, pink and white primroses.

Another fun party game is the "Famous Couple" game. Pin the names of famous couples onto the backs of two guests. Examples: Romeo and Juliet, Mickey and Minnie Mouse, Tom and Jerry, or Batman and Robin. Modify the famous couples according to the age of the guests. The designated "famous couple" can ask questions about who they are, but the other guests can only answer "yes" or "no." Set a time limit. If the pair guesses correctly, they can choose guests to be the next "famous couple."

Set up a Valentine's Day sundae bar. Serve strawberry and vanilla ice cream, a variety of syrups, berries, whipped cream, cherries, and Valentine's Day candies and sprinkles.

Seal cards and letters with heart-shaped stickers or a red or pink lipstick kiss.

Make thumbprint cookies and fill with strawberry jam.

Order red and pink-tinted bread from your local bakery. Cut into heart shapes for sandwiches and toast.

Cut sponges into heart shapes and stamp on valentines, lunch sacks, T-shirts, tennis shoes, note pads, flowerpots, etc. Or have your children dip their thumbs in red or pink washable ink and form heart-shaped stamps. Give these creations as gifts to special friends and family members.

Make a cherry pie. Before baking, cut out pie crust dough into heart shapes, roll in sugar and arrange on top of your pie. Or use a heart-shaped cookie cutter to cut heart shapes from the top crust, letting the cherry red show through.

Draw lips or hearts or write a love message on the bathroom mirror with lipstick or shaving cream.

Set out a basket filled with books about Valentine's Day and love.

Make special Valentine's Day cookies. You will need large and small heart-shaped cookie cutters. Cut out large hearts. Cut out a small heart from half of the large heart cookies. Frost the solid heart with pink or red frosting. Put the second cookie with the cut out heart on top. You will see the colored frosting showing through. Bake the cut-out centers too, decorate and enjoy!

Make a fun Valentine's Day card from poster board. Cut into puzzle pieces before putting into the envelope.

If you have young children, throw a Valentine's Day tea party. Serve heart-shaped sandwiches with strawberry cream cheese and pink tea or punch. Use white paper doilies as place mats on a red tablecloth. For more tea party ideas, see pages 147-149.

Place a Valentine's Day message to someone you love in your local newspaper.

Set up a cupcake decorating station with pink, red, and white frostings. Include conversation-hearts, heart-shaped cinnamon candies, flattened pink or red gumdrops cut into heart shapes, chocolate hearts, red licorice shoelaces, edible glitter and lots of sprinkles. If you want to get really fancy, layer the batter before baking by putting a pink layer, then white, then pink on top. Or make a marbled cupcake by starting with pink or white and swirling in a small amount of red batter. Here's a method for a fool-proof heart design. On newly frosted cupcakes, put a mini heart cookie cutter on top, spoon sprinkles into the center, and remove cutter.

Hang a heart-shaped wreath on your front door with an antique valentine tucked in.

Buy mini cellophane bags decorated with hearts or cupids and fill them with pencils, stickers, and heart-shaped erasers. Set next to your child's bed or place setting or secretly tuck into her school backpack.

Create a Valentine's Day display using items from around your house. Dig out any heart-shaped bowls or picture frames and anything with cupids on it. Put out red or pink candles or tie valentine ribbon around white ones. Dress teddy bears in red sweaters or tie red organdy ribbon around their ears or neck and tuck valentines into their arms. Place a few valentines under clear table-tops and desk blotters.

Create a message using conversation-heart candy. Put them in your child's lunch box and include a note asking him to figure out the secret phrase.

NOTES

NOTES

SPRING

SPRING TRADITIONS

Springtime is the perfect time to hear birds singing. Call your local Audubon Society, city park, or specialty bird shop. Ask for information on guided walks—a fun way to spend an afternoon.

Make baseball cupcakes. Frost with white frosting and pipe on red "stitching." This also works great on cookies when you use a round cookie cutter.

Tuck a dandelion in its seed pod stage (the puffy white balls that are pests in your yard!) into a ribbon on a gift. Attach a note that reads "make a wish."

Take a family outing to a tulip farm. Pack a picnic lunch or go out to a fun restaurant. Let everyone choose his or her favorite tulip variety and order the bulbs. In October, plant the bulbs, identifying each with a marker that includes the family member's name, date and tulip variety. Each year you can look forward to the tulips' splendid return. Imagine how beautiful your spring garden will look!

Display pictures on your refrigerator of your family enjoying spring pastimes.

Keep your child's smallest rubber boots. When the boots are too small to wear, fill with small bedding plants and set on your porch.

Extend the life of beautiful flowers by pressing them. Press flowers between pages of books. First, lay the flowers between sheets of waxed paper to protect the pages, and let the flowers dry for several weeks. Sprinkle the flowers on tablecloths or under clear table tops or desk blotters.

Bring spring indoors. Put fresh flowers into vases, teapots, teacups, etc. all around the house, including the children's bedrooms. If you have plain wreaths or garlands in your home, freshen them with spring flowers. Put small bouquets into plastic water tubes (available at florists) and tuck them into the foliage.

Put clean, edible and pesticide-free flowers on cakes, cupcakes and in salads. You might want to plant a garden of these so they are handy. Try day lily flowers, dianthus, herb blossoms, johnny-jump-ups, pansies, pea and bean blossoms, roses, tuberous begonias and violets.

Another way to enjoy edible flowers is to candy them. Use powdered egg whites (available at grocery stores and cake decorating supply shops) and follow directions for making two egg whites. Dilute with a small amount of warm water and dab onto flowers with fingers or a small paintbrush. Use tweezers to hold the flower in place. Sprinkle superfine granulated sugar over the entire flower (front and back). Place on waxed paper or a wire rack to dry for at least eight hours or until firm. Keep in a padded airtight container.

When giving a gift, tuck a tiny bouquet of flowers into the ribbon.

Plant a children's garden. Let the kids pick out their favorite vegetables and include some new ones. Look for interesting varieties such as "Easter Egg" radishes, which come in lavender, white and pink as well as red. Another idea: plant a garden with all miniature or giant-sized varieties of vegetables and flowers.

Play baseball until dark and then switch to a glow-in-the-dark ball and play until after dark!

Keep a journal of your gardening successes and mistakes. If they are interested, pass this on to your children when they have their own gardens. Give them cuttings from your yard to include in theirs.

Spend a windy afternoon flying kites.

Buy your children their own gardening tools and gloves. If you want to have a fun heirloom, buy the metal tools. When the kids outgrow them, you can bring out the tools and use them to decorate with at springtime. That is, until the kids want the tools back!

Plant a butterfly garden. Buy the seeds in a shaker can or pick your own plants. Some varieties are: bee balm, butterfly bush, cosmos, honeysuckle, lantana, nasturtiums, oregano and zinnias. Have a picnic on the grass and enjoy the beauty.

Tuck a fresh flower into each napkin ring.

Enjoy watching humming-birds. Hang a feeder by the kitchen window.

NOTES

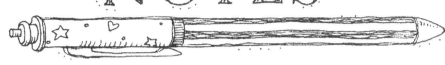

NOTES

St. Patrick's Day

Surprise your kids with a St. Patrick's Day lunch. Call your local bagel shop and order green bagels a few days in advance. Tint cream cheese, include green apples with caramel dip, a green boxed juice, and put in a holiday napkin. Don't forget to decorate the bag with lots of shamrocks!

For a fun activity, pick clover and tie together to form a necklace. *Note*: Clover is not a member of the shamrock family, but it looks similar, it's easy to find, and you can't beat the price!

Have a treasure hunt for gold-wrapped chocolate coins. Or if you really want to be creative, add a few real Irish coins. Call around to your local coin shops and find out who has bronze-colored Irish coins. Some shops offer a rummage section where you can pick up some coins for as little as 10 cents each. This will make your hunt very magical—who else but genuine leprechauns could have left them?

I R I S H

Key Idea

Play IRISH bingo with green jelly beans or gold coins for markers.

2

8

1

5

chocolate coin.
5¢

23

chocolate coin.
5¢

29

7

15

9

chocolate coin.
25¢

chocolate coin.
25¢

11

chocolate coin.
25¢

14

10

18

🥣 Make an all-green dinner. Items that are easily tinted green with a little help from food coloring are milk, mashed potatoes, apple-sauce, rice and homemade bread (tint the dough before baking). Just a hint: Tinting butter doesn't work!

🥣 Make shamrock cupcakes. Cut out a shamrock stencil. Frost your cupcakes or cake with white or light green frosting. Put the stencil over the soft frosting, spoon in dark green sprinkles and remove the stencil.

🥣 Put green food coloring in scrambled eggs, oatmeal, milk for cereal, white muffin mix or pancake batter for St. Patrick's Day breakfast.

🥣 Serve lime sherbet, or pistachio pudding for dessert.

🥣 Frost cupcakes with a rainbow design and top each with a gold-wrapped choco-late coin to represent the pot of gold at the end of the rainbow.

🥣 Children in Ireland cele-brate St. Patrick's Day by enjoying a healthy holiday meal. You might like to try this with your family. Cook kale and add to mashed potatoes. If your children are old enough, add quarters, nickels and dimes wrapped in foil. Before eating, they get to dig through the potatoes on their plates and find the money. Put cooked carrots on the plate also and you'll have the colors of the Irish flag.
Note: This is not appropri-ate for very young children. Make sure everyone finds the coins first to avoid choking.

🥣 Tint pizza dough green before baking.

 Sprinkle green shamrock confetti on your kitchen table and in lunch boxes.

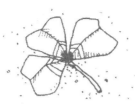

Serve an all-green vegetable tray. Include broccoli, celery (if you like, fill with green-tinted cream cheese), green beans, cucumbers, snap peas, asparagus, or any other family favorites. Cut the top off a green pepper and hollow out, now you have a bowl in the shape of a shamrock. Fill with tinted dip.

Fill clear cellophane bags with green jelly beans, tie with foil shamrock garland and put at each place setting.

Make St. Patrick's Day-style chicken pot pies. Before baking, dye some or all of the dough green. If you want only a small accent, make the regular color crust and top with a green shamrock shape cut out of the scraps, which you've tinted green.

Make chocolate-chip-mint milkshakes for dessert and insert a chunky green straw.

Potatoes are a traditional Irish favorite. Serve a potato bar for dinner with a variety of toppings.

Play "Hot Potato." Wrap a cold potato in foil and pass it around fast. If you drop it, you're out. Give out gold-wrapped chocolate coins to the winners.

Make shamrock cookies. Set them out on a special plate or use to decorate cupcakes or cakes.

For a fun lunch, secretly tint mayonnaise green before making sandwiches.

Serve a traditional Irish dish like Irish stew, corned beef and cabbage, or home-made soda bread.

Make a green punch by combining 7 UP® and softened lime sherbet.

NOTES

NOTES

Easter

The day before Easter, start a family tradition of preparing a special bread or rolls. Make cinnamon rolls, bear claws or other favorite. Let them rise overnight. The kids will be proud when the goodies come out of the oven on Easter morning, and what a wonderful smell to wake up to! Or you could make traditional hot cross buns for dinner. If your family doesn't care for the candied fruit, substitute nuts, raisins and any favorite dried fruits.

If you have saved anything from your childhood—for example, your Easter basket, an Easter book, or small stuffed bunny, incorporate that into your decorations. Purchase a few keepsake items or a special basket for your children that they can take with them when they leave home.

Play BUNNY bingo and use jelly beans or other seasonal candy for markers.

The day before Easter, mow the back lawn and leave the clippings. The next morning form the clippings into nests for eggs and other fun surprises.

If you have a young daughter, consider this heirloom idea. Each year on Easter, tie a different pastel ribbon in your daughter's hair. After Easter is over, tie the ribbon on her basket. When she gets older she will have a basket full of beauty and memories.

Decorate your cakes and cupcakes with edible Easter "grass." Dye almond paste green and squeeze through a garlic press.

Decorate your home for Easter with things found in nature, or that look realistic. Use nests, potted spring flowers, grasses, moss, vegetable starts, etc. Intermix with your decorated eggs. Add candy eggs or chocolate foil-wrapped spring animals, as well as other favorite Easter decorations.

Make chocolate chip cookies—substitute pastel M&M's® brand chocolate candies for the chocolate chips before baking.

Bake a three-layer cake. Put a different pastel color of frosting between each layer.

Make chick or carrot cupcakes. Line cupcake tins with pastel paper liners. For chicks: Make lemon cupcakes with white frosting. Take a mini chick cookie cutter and place on top. With a small spoon fill in with bright yellow sugar sprinkles and remove. For carrots: Make carrot cake filling. Use a mini carrot cookie cutter with bright orange and green sprinkles. A plate of these would make a charming addition to any holiday table.

Have an egg rolling contest (a tradition at the White House). Set up a "START" and a "FINISH" line. Give each child a hard-boiled egg and a small stick or wooden spoon. Have them push the egg to the finish line without breaking it. Make it a race, a relay race, or set up an obstacle course.

Fill clear lamp bases with pastel speckled eggs, jelly beans, or miniature foil-wrapped eggs, bunnies, chicks or carrots.

Set up an Easter cookie decorating station. Put out small bowls with powdered sugar mixed with a small amount of heavy cream. Or as an alternative, dilute canned vanilla frosting with a little water or milk. Add a variety of food colorings, place a paintbrush in each color and have fun! *Note*: For a great selection of food coloring, go to a cake decorating supply shop.

Visit your local fine candy store and see if they have anything wonderful to decorate with. My mother found a two-foot-high white chocolate bunny carrying a basket of colored eggs. She stores this in a safe place and uses it as a centerpiece each year. She has had to re-glue a few eggs, but other than that it's perfect, and it wouldn't be Easter without this on the table!

To create a springtime look for your Easter table, make marzipan ladybugs, bees, bunnies, chicks, carrots, or any other vegetable or critter. To tint: Dip the end of a toothpick into a soft shade of paste food coloring and knead into marzipan.

Incorporate these edible creations into your center-piece, or put one at each place setting. Another idea: decorate a cake or cupcakes with miniature designs.

Make Easter basket cupcakes. Frost cupcakes with white frosting. Dye coconut with green food coloring and sprinkle on top to form a nest. Add mini jelly beans, small chicks, bunnies or any other small seasonal candy. Use a pipe cleaner to form a handle and tie on a pretty ribbon. Another version is doing the same thing to a cake. This idea has been around forever but is still thoroughly enjoyed.

eggs

Make a fun family activity out of dyeing eggs. Your options are unlimited. There are many boxed kits and food coloring products available, or try natural dyes. To make a natural dye, add 2 cups of natural ingredients to a saucepan and fill with just enough water to cover the material. Add 2 Tablespoons of vinegar. If you are planning to make hard-boiled eggs, boil the egg in the pigment material for 10 minutes. If you want to use the eggs for decorations and will be blowing out the egg contents, cool the solution first and immerse the egg for 30 minutes or longer for desired color.

Remove eggs from dye and dry on paper towels. If you want a shiny coating, polish them with a little cooking oil.

Chicken eggs are always a favorite and are readily available. If you would like to decorate with a variety of sizes and natural colors, check out gourmet shops and Asian grocery stores. You may have to call several places, but try to find duck, goose, pheasant and quail eggs.

Two things to remember:

If you are planning to eat your egg, make sure the dye is edible, just in case it leaks onto the egg. Also, use a saucepan that will not stain.

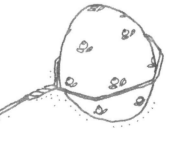

Listed below are some colors to try, or experiment to come up with your own natural colors.

Blue . . . . Blueberries

Robin's egg blue . . . Red cabbage

Brown . . . . 1 T. of instant coffee dissolved in 2/3 cup of hot water, add 1/2 t. vinegar.

Green . . . . Spinach. You can also dip a yellow egg in blue dye.

Lavender . . . . Grape juice

Pink . . . . Cranberry juice or pickled or shredded raw beets

Red . . . . Red onions. Add 2 cups of water and boil for ½ to 1 hour.

Tan . . . . Brown onion skins, or shells from a dozen walnuts

Violet-Blue . . . . Violet blossoms. Cover with hot water and let sit overnight.

Yellow . . . . 1 t. to 2 T. turmeric depending on hue. Add 2/3 cup of hot water and 1/4 t. vinegar.

Note: T.=Tablespoon and t.=teaspoon

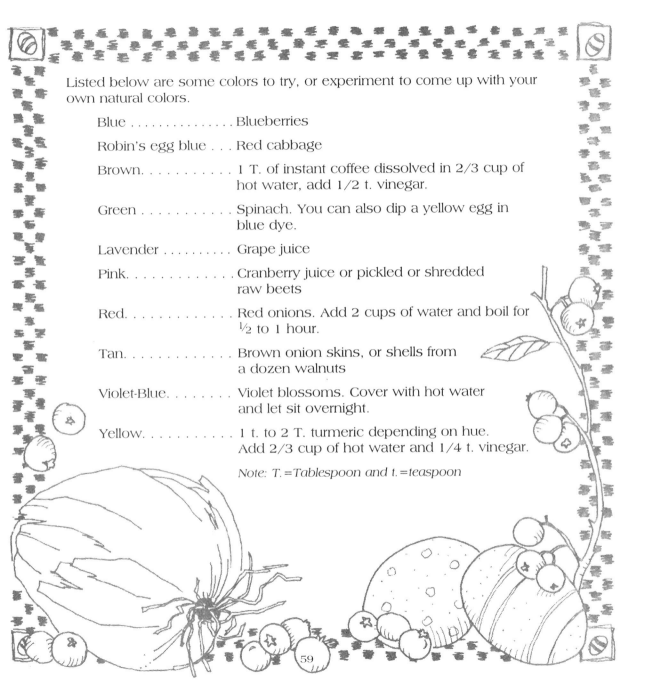

There are so many ways to embellish eggs. If you want a keepsake, you will need to blow out the raw eggs. Make a small hole with a needle in both ends of the egg. Blow contents into a bowl. This is fun to do as a family. If your children are smaller, chances are you will need to help them get it started. You can also purchase tools that are designed for egg blowing, or use a rubber suction bulb, which is available in the infant's section of the drug store. When contents are blown out, rinse out the shell under running water and dry.

Note: Remember, if using a hard-boiled egg, do not use decorating materials that are non-edible. For example, glue and paint may seep onto the egg.

Consider some of the following decorations:

- Stickers. Put on small stickers in desired shapes or create sayings with small stick-on letters. Dip eggs in dye, remove stickers while still wet and easy to take off. The covered area will remain white when the stickers are removed.

- Wrinkle up a 9-inch piece of plastic kitchen wrap and place the egg in the center. Wrap tightly by twisting the sides together. Dip in dye, some will seep under the plastic, creating a unique design. Unwrap to dry.

- Wrap rubber bands around the egg before dyeing. Let dry before removing bands. Or try putting bands around the middle portions, and dip the ends in different colors, keeping the middle white.

- Dip eggs in water, remove and cover with different colors of torn up tissue paper. Allow to dry and remove paper. This gives the eggs a soft colored pattern.

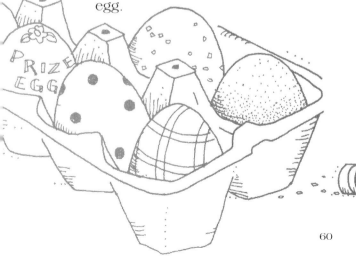

- Break up a colorful variety of dyed egg shells into small pieces and glue onto another egg to create a mosaic look.

- Write on an egg with a white crayon, a small birthday candle, or etch in a design with a needle.

- Sponge paint eggs with paints or food-safe dye.

- Stick on tape in vertical and horizontal strips to form a plaid design. When dry, peel off tape.

- Dip a cotton swab in petroleum jelly and scribble on a design or name. Dip in dye. When dry, wipe off jelly.

- When you have your beautifully colored and dried egg, glue on colored plastic gemstones, small fabric flowers or trimming.

For a beautifully decorated egg, use delicately shaped flowers or other greenery. Place the veined side of the flower or leaf against the egg. Wrap in a square piece of pantyhose and tie tightly at the back. Put into dye for desired color. Let egg dry completely before removing fabric and flower or greenery.

Make sugar-coated eggs. Brush the surface of the blown-out egg with craft glue and roll in colored sugar. To make colored sugar, fill a lidded container with one cup of sugar. Add a few drops of gel food coloring and shake until evenly colored. Pour out onto waxed paper and roll eggs.

When you are done decorating your hand-blown eggs, put clear glue over the holes to prevent the eggs from cracking further. Sign and date them each year. To safely store your new family heirlooms, place them in an empty egg carton.

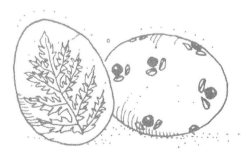

BASKETS

Some items to add to Easter baskets in addition to what the Easter Bunny leaves:

Art supplies:

• Rubber stamps, ink pads, markers, and an assortment of cards, paper and envelopes

• A variety of paintbrushes in bright colors, tubes of paint or paintboxes, paper, a rolled up paint shirt for smaller kids, or more advanced supplies for older children

• Bright colored pencils, sketch pads and a "How to Draw" book

Sports:

Fill a baseball cap with trading cards, a new softball, a rolled-up T-shirt and chocolate wrapped mini baseballs.

Travel activities:

• Hand-held small electronic games, cards, travel games, word search or crossword puzzle books, small books, tapes or CDs. You could even roll up a small travel pillow. Shred a map instead of Easter grass.

• Smile! Insert an inexpensive camera, small photo album, and film hidden inside a plastic egg. This would be especially great for a child heading off to camp or a vacation in the future.

Gardening:

Packaged in a terra cotta pot or basket, put in kid-size gardening gloves, seed packets, kid-size tools, and chocolates in the shapes of flowers, insects or vegetables.

Beach:

Fill a sand pail with bright, shredded paper. Put in sand toys, foil-wrapped candy shells and fish, sunglasses, and a small stuffed crab toy. For an older child, expand on this theme.

- Girls: Put shredded paper or bright colored tissue in a clear beach bag. Add sunglasses, suntan products, a magazine, and some fun candy.
- Boys: Roll up a beach towel and stuff the shredded paper in the top; or, fill a mini cooler with sunglasses, suntan products, colorful candy, and sporting goods.

Bath:

Fill a basket with bath products. Tie colorful cellophane and ribbons around bubble bath, fun shaped bath beads or soaps, and lotions. Put in a brightly colored bath mitt for a younger child.

An older child might enjoy a bath pillow, bath sponge, or scented candle.

Use your imagination and consider a variety of containers and use brightly colored shredded papers. Some choices might be:

- Bike helmet
- Water bottle
- Small picnic basket
- Small tote, athletic, travel or cosmetic bag

If you don't choose to put together a theme basket, there are many fillers you could use! Some items might include:

- Kite, jump rope, balls, or any other outdoor activity
- Children's magazine with subscription coupon
- Whimsically patterned socks
- Small wind-up toys
- Small stuffed animals or plastic animals
- Small books
- Jewelry or items to make jewelry
- Cassettes or CDs
- Small toy boats, cars, or airplanes

Key Idea

Hang brightly colored plastic Easter eggs from the branches of trees in your front yard.

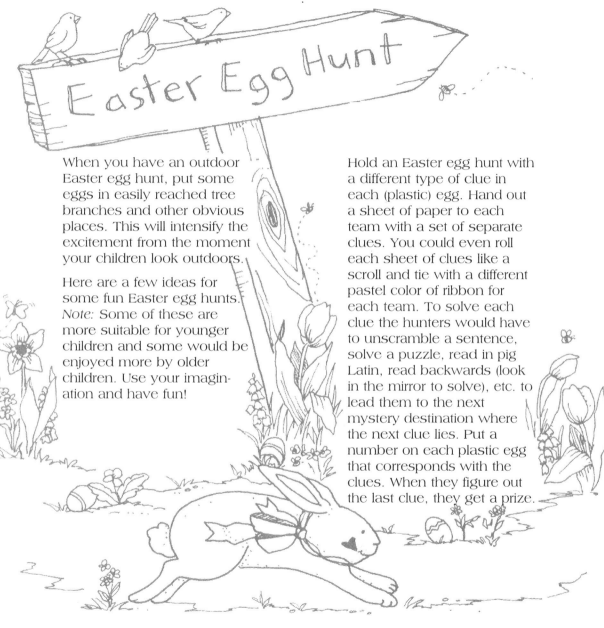

Easter Egg Hunt

When you have an outdoor Easter egg hunt, put some eggs in easily reached tree branches and other obvious places. This will intensify the excitement from the moment your children look outdoors.

Here are a few ideas for some fun Easter egg hunts. *Note:* Some of these are more suitable for younger children and some would be enjoyed more by older children. Use your imagination and have fun!

Hold an Easter egg hunt with a different type of clue in each (plastic) egg. Hand out a sheet of paper to each team with a set of separate clues. You could even roll each sheet of clues like a scroll and tie with a different pastel color of ribbon for each team. To solve each clue the hunters would have to unscramble a sentence, solve a puzzle, read in pig Latin, read backwards (look in the mirror to solve), etc. to lead them to the next mystery destination where the next clue lies. Put a number on each plastic egg that corresponds with the clues. When they figure out the last clue, they get a prize.

Hold an Easter egg hunt for older kids and teach them how to read a compass. Pass out compasses, which make fine keepsakes. Explain how to use and read the compass. Let the kids break into teams, each with a different set of clues (for example, set the compass to 75 degrees NE and walk 22 steps –or– set the compass to 30 degrees east and walk 10 steps). Each clue will then take the team to the next direction, eventually leading to a hidden prize. This works best outdoors.

Have an Easter egg hunt for jelly beans, each color meaning a specific value. This works particularly well for inside hunts. You could also make a trail with jelly beans. Give each child a small basket or container and have them follow the trail to a surprise.

Have a "golden" egg hidden as a special prize. It could be a gold foil-wrapped chocolate egg, or a giant plastic egg sprayed gold or wrapped in gold foil. Fill the plastic egg with goodies and/or money. To make it extra magical, wrap with gold star garland as well. If you have several younger children, you might want to hide one for each.

If you have older children, have a flashlight egg hunt. This can be done indoors or outdoors. Use glow-in-the-dark markers or paint to mark the eggs. Have participants use their own flashlights or hand out pastel ones as gifts.

For the younger kids, organize a game where they get to play "Easter Bunny." Let the kids create an Easter basket filled with "goodies" (stickers). To play: Give each child a piece of construction paper cut into the shape of a basket with a handle. On the back of the basket, put an assortment of stickers in the shapes of Easter goodies to find. Hide plastic eggs containing the matching stickers. When the kids find all the matching stickers, they get to put the found stickers on the front of their baskets. Remember, if they discover an egg with a sticker they've already found, have them sneak it back for someone else to find. *Note:* a great source of stickers is a scrapbook supply store.

Get together with your neighbors and start a tradition of having an Easter egg hunt the Saturday before Easter. This is a great way to create childhood memories and at the same time get better acquainted with your neighbors. This works great if you have a neighborhood park, or take turns at each others houses. The kids can help fill the eggs and everyone can get involved.

NOTES

NOTES

NOTES

May Day

♡ Remember the people who are important to you—family, friends or neighbors who might not have small children in their lives.

🎁 Make a paper cone out of a solid color of construction paper, or weave two colors of paper strips together to create a basket effect. Decorate and attach a ribbon handle. Fill with anything your heart desires. Get creative! Here are some suggestions:

- Fresh flowers. To keep flowers fresh until morning, pick up some small water tubes at your local florist.

- Seed packets glued onto popsicle sticks and put inside to form a bouquet. If you wish, you can glue on paper petals.

- Small flower-shaped cookies wrapped in cellophane and tied with a pretty ribbon.

- Paper flowers cut out of stiff, bright paper. Use pinking shears or other interesting-edged scissors. Tape a crazy-shaped straw to the back for a stem. You might even want to glue on a foil-wrapped chocolate in a bug or butterfly shape.

Key Idea

Freeze edible flowers in ice cube trays. Fill each cube halfway with water, place flowers and freeze. Then fill each to the top and freeze again.

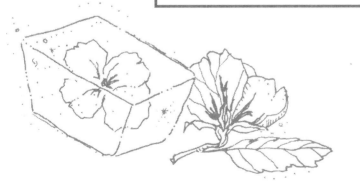

🎁 Plant your favorite bedding plant in a small basket. Tie on a gift tag with a checkered ribbon.

🎁 Wrap a small primrose, pansy, geranium, or other seasonal potted plant in brightly colored tissue paper or cellophane. Tuck in a small handmade garden sign that reads "Happy May Day."

👄 Now the fun begins!

. . . Wait until dark and the kids are in their pajamas. Load everyone in the car with their secret May Day surprises. Drive around your neighborhood and when you arrive at your children's friends or other special recipient's home, pull up close by and shut off your car headlights.

. . . Quietly open the car door and let the kids sneak out. Have them hang the May baskets on door handles or set them on the porch. Then the kids quietly run back to the car, shut the door and you take off. Guaranteed to bring smiles to your children's' faces as well as the lucky finder's.

🎁 Another fun and sneaky thing to do is to surprise someone special with a small May Day garden. Grandparents especially would be delighted to wake up and find their empty planter box or small garden brimming with bright flowers!

Make individual flower-pot desserts. Fill small, new plastic flowerpots (the plastic ones that look like terra cotta are especially cute) with rocky road ice cream. Top with fudge sauce and choco-late cookie crumbs. Decorate with flowers made from flattened gumdrops, add gummy worms and other kinds of colorful "garden variety" candy.

Surprise the special people in your life with flowers in their bedrooms.

Make your own flower confetti. Use bright-colored paper and a flower paper punch. Sprinkle on your tablecloth or in May Day cards or lunch boxes.

Paint a tiny flower on your child's cheek.

Bake bread in flower-shaped bread tubes.

Make May Day cupcakes. After baking, cool then frost and decorate with sugared flowers (see page 45). Set the cupcake in the center of a small round paper doily. Form it around the cupcake liner to simulate a lacy basket and secure with a ribbon. Bend a piece of pipe cleaner and poke it into the top of the cupcake for a handle.

Set your table in a May Day theme. Cut out large daisy-shaped flowers out of bright vinyl fabric with pinking shears (or use heavy paper for a one-time use). These make great placemats that can be used year after year. Use different colored paper plates to look like the middle of the flowers.

NOTES

NOTES

Mother's Day

♡ The best gift you can give on Mother's Day is the gift of love. Spend time with your mom and let her know you appreciate her!

☞ Check around and see what local activities will be offered for Mother's Day well in advance. She will not feel special if you are scrambling around the last minute to find something to do.

♡ Listen to mother's wishes when planning her special day. She might not want to spend an afternoon at the zoo, when she is hoping to spend the day working in the garden.

🎁 Surprise mom with a quiet retreat in her own bathroom. First, make sure that it's clean! Bring in a scented candle, flowers, new magazines or a book, a cold drink and a portable stereo with soothing music. You could purchase some pampering bath products or hang a new nightgown or robe on the door. The most important part would be a sign on the door reading "JUST FOR MOM . . . PLEASE DO NOT DISTURB!"

🎁 Does your mom love flowers? Buy her a beautiful rose bush or other flowers that can be cut and enjoyed all summer (be sure to volunteer to plant them for her). You might buy her a special vase to put the flowers in.

Best mom

🎁 If you are the mother of small children, have them decorate a hat box, small trunk or other lidded box. This would make a perfect container for all of the treasures the kids make throughout the year . . . but, of course, use only when the works aren't on display!

♡ Older kids can surprise mom by doing all the chores for the day. This is mom's day to be pampered.

🎁 Bring an old picture back to life. Find an old black-and-white photo of yourself as a young child doing something special with your mother. Bring it in to a photographer who does custom work. Have them make a copy and hand-tint areas on the photo by doing a color wash in soft pastel colors. Now you have a keepsake that is also a work of art. Make sure you bring this in for processing several months in advance.

🐁 One way to spend time alone with your mom is by giving her a coupon for a special outing for just the two of you. This might be for a sporting event, a play, a tea, a bike ride, or any other activity that you both would enjoy. Don't forget your camera to document your memorable day.

🥣 Surprise her with a special breakfast. Set the table with her best dishes, or serve her breakfast in bed.

🎁 Create a year 'round video for a special mom documenting her child's life. Set it to music and include milestones and other special moments throughout the year. Every year on Mother's Day she could sit down and watch it with her child. This is a gift her children will enjoy as much as she. Another thought: Create an ongoing scrapbook or photo album.

NOTES

SUMMER

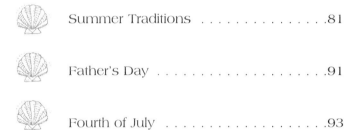

SUMMER TRADITIONS

♡ Remember all the excitement that summer held for you as a child . . . playing at the beach, running through the sprinkler, catching your first fish, camping, etc. If you can find pictures of yourself and your spouse enjoying those wonderful memories as children, display them. Recapture that excitement by reliving those activities with your children.

Stock up on library books, find a warm sunny spot and indulge yourself!

Start a fun family tradition out of picking up a souvenir magnet each year on your vacation. Use the magnets on your refrigerator to display pictures of your family enjoying summer pastimes.

Put a big terra cotta pot filled with geraniums on your kitchen table.

Make homemade ice cream bars. Cut ice cream (from a rectangular carton) into small square or rectangular shapes. Place on a cookie sheet and freeze until firm. Insert popsicle sticks, spread on a fudgy-chocolate ice cream coating and dot with your favorite candies or pieces of your favorite candy bar. Enjoy right away or wrap in foil and freeze until firm.

Replace the soaps seasonally in your bathrooms. In summer use crab, bee, fish, frog, shell and sun-shaped soaps.

♡ If you have kids in elementary school, just before summer vacation, take pictures of the memorable people and places of your child's school year. For example: your child in line with schoolmates, playing four-square at recess, or with their teachers. Make sure you check with your child so it's not too embarrassing!

🎁 When giving summer gifts, use a summer motif. For wrapping paper, try sky blue tissue paper and stamp with yellow suns, or use a red and white checkered paper tablecloth. Tie packages with sheer ribbons featuring garden or other summer designs for instant summer charm. Look for unique summer confetti to sprinkle in cards.

🥢 Purchase a variety of lawn sprinklers to bring out on a hot summer day. When the excitement of the sprinklers has worn off for your kids, bring out a new supply of squirt guns. Have on hand clean buckets, all ready to be filled.

🥢 Collect seashells to paint on another day.

🥣 If you are having a large gathering or family reunion, try this idea: In your invitation ask each person to design a lunch. Lunch could be packed in a sand pail, a basket, a box, or a decorated bag, for example. Set all the lunch packages out on your table and let each person choose one.

🥢 Set up an outdoor art studio. Let the kids be as creative and messy as they want! Set up a finger painting station or containers of paint and nice, big brushes. For young children, set out a big bucket of clean water and a bunch of paintbrushes and let them "paint" on the concrete or deck.

🥣 Make lemonade from scratch. To make 2 quarts, you will need:
   8 lemons
   1 cup of sugar (or to taste)
   8 cups of ice cold water
Cut the lemons into thin slices and remove the seeds. Place in the bottom of your pitcher and pour in the sugar. Using a masher or long-handled spoon, press the lemons until juicy. Add water and stir. Remove lemons and enjoy! Encourage your kids to set up a lemonade stand.

For a fun outing, go berry picking and make homemade jam or pies that night. If you make jam, put on a label that will remind everyone of their fun day.

Make an easy berry picking container out of a plastic milk jug. Leaving the handle in tact, cut a triangular shape out of the top and front (it will look like a big scoop with sides). Tie a string around the handle and put around your neck to free your hands for picking. Make sure you wear an old shirt!

One evening, bring out old vacation photographs and video tapes and remember the fun times!

Fill clear lamp bases with sea glass and seashells.

Think ahead to what you would like to see in your fall garden. Plant corn, pumpkins and sunflowers in early summer. If you decide to plant sunflowers, take advantage of a great photo opportunity. Take a picture of your child or children planting the sunflowers. Then during the four-month growing period, take subsequent pictures of the young gardeners alongside the sunflowers, until the flowers are in full bloom. Frame the sequence and enjoy each fall. *Note:* see "Autumn Traditions" pages 107 & 108 for additional contests and decorating ideas.

Roast marshmallows and make s'mores. Experiment with different flavored graham crackers, a variety of thin candy bars, and other additions, such as peanut butter. Think about your favorite flavors and come up with your own recipes. Name your creations, and enjoy them each summer.

MILK 1%

Key Idea

Make "sand dollar" sugar cookies. Insert five almonds pointing to the center and sprinkle with cinnamon and sugar "sand" before baking.

Purchase a shaved ice machine and enjoy home-made snow cones all summer. Use melted juice concentrates for the syrups.

Keep your picnic basket well stocked so you can take lunch or dinner to the beach or park at a moment's notice. In the basket put a blanket, plastic food containers, plates, cups, silverware, napkins, small salt and pepper shakers and a trash bag. Keep a small cooler within easy access.

Just for fun . . . purchase some miniature black plastic ants. Sprinkle them around on your red checkered table-cloth, to add a little "charac-ter" to your casual outside dinner party.

Set up a tent in your backyard and have a spur-of-the-moment camp out. Eat dinner outside, read by flashlight, and enjoy the free show of stars.

Make one-of-a-kind vacation frames. When you are on your summer trip, pick up small souvenirs like found natural objects, paper scraps (from napkins, brochures, ticket stubs, matchbook covers, etc.), or any other small trinkets.

For example, if you vacation at the beach, take a small zip-lock bag and put in some sand, small shells, sea glass, even a small rolled up umbrella from someone's exotic drink. When you get home, you could always purchase miniature "vaca-tion" items and add a small pair of sunglasses, sandals, or anything else that would remind you of your trip.

Buy a plain frame and have fun decorating it with all your "treasures." Put in your favorite picture (be sure to take a lot so you can have a choice). Make a new frame each year.

It's not too early to be thinking of your Christmas card! Your family vacation is a great time to snap a family picture. Have fun with it! For example, if at the beach you could do any of the following: Write "Happy Holidays!" in the sand and take a group picture; bury everyone in the sand (this would require some outside help), have someone put a Santa hat on each and snap the picture; or how about building a snowman out of sand, complete with sunglasses, baseball cap, swim fins, shell buttons . . . who knows? It may sound crazy, but it will bring a good smile at Christmas!

For a special treat on a warm summer evening, make homemade ice cream after dinner. Choose a fresh summer fruit or use any other favorite flavoring. Buy an old-fashioned crank-style ice cream maker and let everyone take a turn.

Plant a cutting garden full of fragrant flowers. Put small potted tomato and strawberry plants on your back porch — enjoy all the scents and flavors of summer.

Make beach cupcakes. After baking and cooling, frost and immediately sprinkle on finely crushed vanilla wafer crumbs for "sand." Add a paper umbrella, gummy fish, candy shells, etc.

Eat outside whenever possible. Set up an inviting outdoor dining area that is ready to use. For entertaining, in addition to candlelight, string lights in the trees or nearby bushes.

Play a rousing game of badminton or croquet. If your croquet mallet is too long for a young child to use, substitute your plunger handle.

🐦 Enjoy your own backyard. Run around barefoot, lie on the grass and enjoy a picnic lunch, make whistles with blades of grass and look for four-leaf clovers. Make an instant secret clubhouse or fort by tying a rope between two trees and draping a sheet or blanket over it.

🐦 Are you looking for a memorable vacation destination that is different than an amusement park or beach? Call your local travel agent for unique ideas. Have you ever considered renting an RV, spending a week on a houseboat, staying on a ranch or farm, renting a cabin in the woods, or spending the night in a covered wagon or caboose? It's going to be hard to choose from your many options!

🐦 Buy each of your children a small photo album and let them pick out a postcard from each vacation stop.

🐦 If you are planning to spend a lot of time in your car this summer, keep it well stocked with activities. Fill a small box with travel games along with playing cards, note pads, and colored pencils or pens. If you are going on a car trip, try playing one of these fun games:

- One person thinks of a word, for example, VACATION. Each person writes the word on their note pad. Try to locate the letters in the word from license plates, road signs or businesses. As you find each letter, cross it off. The first person to find all the letters in the word wins and gets to choose the next word.

- Play an alphabet game. Have one person pick a topic, for example, food items. Starting with the letter "A" apple, the next person picks a food starting with "B" and so on. Try to go as fast as you can through the alphabet without stopping.

Take your family on an adventure while teaching them about goal setting. For example, for good behavior and completion of chores, children could earn reward stickers that they put on a chart. When the chart becomes full, they earn a mystery outing.

Transform your picnic basket into a "mystery outing" basket. Fill your basket the night before, so everyone will have a surprise in the morning. Also, fill a small cooler with drinks and snacks to have either in the car or to carry along . . . that will depend on your destination. And, of course, bring your camera! Here are just a few suggestions of special destinations:

- The Zoo:

    Pack a small backpack, a box of animal crackers, binoculars, and a small amount of money for each child for a "treat," maybe a small souvenir or an ice cream cone. Put in their favorite small zoo stuffed animals as a hint.

- A Pool:

    Pack all your usual swim wear and gear. Include sunscreen, magazines, books, and if the pool allows, floats, toys and small items which your kids can dive for.

    For a fun game to play in the pool, try this version of "Red Light, Green Light." The person who is "It" goes to one end of the pool and everyone else goes to the other end. "It" gets to choose the category, for example, animals, types of candy, or fruit. Everyone else picks something from the category, keeping it to themselves. "It" starts calling out related items, for example, if the category is animals, he could start saying "cat, dog, horse," etc. If you chose cat, you would slowly start swimming or walking toward "It" as quietly as possible. If "It" hears a noise, he can turn around and tag you if you are moving. The object of the game is to sneak up and tag "It" before he tags you!

- Take a nature hike:

Pack a backpack, small binoculars, a small bug house or lidded jar (poke holes in advance), compass, magnifying glass and some books on bugs and birds. Choose a destination that has a well-marked trail.

A caterpillar hike is really fun. Form a line and have each person put both hands on the shoulders of the person in front of them. Everybody closes their eyes except the leader. The leader calls out a command such as, "straight ahead," "turn left," "go over the stick," "duck your head," etc. Each person in turn, repeats and follows the command. After a pre-determined number of commands, the next person in line becomes the leader.

Scavenger hunts are always popular. You will need to pack small bags and a list of items to collect. Some things might be: a wildflower, a flat rock, three kinds of leaves, a feather, etc. See who can find all the items first! You can use these items on your vacation frames (see page 85).

Extend your fun by collecting items to be used on another day. Collect small pine cones to be glued onto a small plain frame, wildflowers for pressing, rocks for painting, etc. Another fun activity is to make a homemade sling-shot. Look for a small, sturdy forked branch ("Y") and securely tie a thick rubber band that has been cut to each arm. Choose an open area, away from animals and people, possibly your back-yard. Set up a row of small tin cans on a table for practice. Be careful and determine what's behind your target if your missile should miss its mark.

Caution: Trees or shrubs behind your target might not be sufficient. Shoot against something solid, like a sturdy cardboard box or piece of wood.

NOTES

FATHER'S DAY

♡ Let dad choose how he would like to spend his day. He might like to go on a family outing, or his choice might be to go golfing with his friends. Whichever it is, support it enthusiastically! If he is going to be gone for the day, spend that time preparing or purchasing items to make his favorite meal. Involve the whole family in a really special evening.

⌂ Make a Father's Day banner and add to it each year. Sign and date each new addition.

🎁 Buy dad a gift certificate to his favorite bookstore, hardware or sporting goods store. Think of some place where he wouldn't ordinarily spend money on himself, but would love to.

🎁 Purchase a double frame and create a generation picture. Put a picture of your husband sharing a special moment with his father, as a child. Snap some secret pictures of your husband doing the same activity, if possible, with his children. (Hint: If the original photo is black and white, use black and white film.)

🎁 Older kids might give dad a well-deserved day off. Take over his least-favorite chores, wash the car, mow the lawn, take out the garbage, etc. Or make a coupon book, each coupon denotes a chore and dad can present a coupon at a later date.

🥣 Make hero sandwiches for lunch and stick in small toothpick signs saying "We love you" and "Our Hero."

NOTES

Fourth of July

Go flag crazy! Fly your flag several days in advance, or tuck one into a wreath on the front door. Incorporate them into your Fourth of July meal by sticking mini flags into the tops of brownies, cupcakes, hamburger or hot dog buns. For an instant centerpiece, fill pottery crocks or vases with small flags or add them to pots filled with flowers.

Make a plate of star-studded sandwiches by cutting the bread first with a star cookie cutter, or by baking bread in a star-shaped bread tube.

Make "firecracker" treats by filling tall, clear plastic glasses with alternating layers of regular and red-tinted popcorn. Insert a peppermint stick for the "wick" and finish it off by wrapping small pieces of star garland around the top so that it fans out like sparks.

Fill a bucket with red, white, and blue water balloons. Choose a partner and play catch, moving back a step each time you successfully complete a pass. See which team can move back the furthest without their balloon bursting!

Independence Day is a great opportunity to take candid photographs. Snap some shots of your family and friends at a picnic, watching a parade, standing at the fireworks counter, holding a lit sparkler, playing softball, or whatever your family traditionally enjoys. Try to capture the fun of the moment on film.

When serving Fourth of July drinks, put in three thin straws: one red, one white and one blue.

Fill clear lamp bases with flag taffy, red, white and blue M&Ms® brand chocolate candies, jelly beans or other Fourth of July candies.

For a fun treat, dip red licorice sticks into melted white chocolate and shake on blue sprinkles. Set upright in a glass until firm.

Decorate a large rectangular platter with red, white and blue-sprinkled cupcakes positioned to form a flag pattern.

Use red, white and blue bandannas for napkins as well as napkin rings by tying them around individual place settings of silverware. Tuck a mini flag into each.

Make a pie with red and blue berries. Before baking, cut star shapes with a cookie cutter out of the top crust.

Happy Birthday, America! Put a red, a white and a blue candle in each decorated cupcake. Or use sparkler-style candles on top of your Fourth of July cake.

Attend an old-fashioned Fourth of July parade or help organize a neighborhood one. It could be as simple or elaborate as you wish. Give out ribbons or prizes for the best decorated bike, the funniest outfit, the person or pet that is most patriotic, etc. Kids might make their own instruments to play, or ask neighbors who can play instruments to join the parade. Another idea: Play patriotic songs loudly on a boom box as everyone marches along. End the parade at a neighborhood picnic site.

Use clean red, white and blue sand pails as bowls for serving on your Fourth of July table.

Make flag cupcakes or a flag cake. Pipe red frosting stripes onto white frosting. Finish off by creating your blue square with blue frosting or blue sprinkles and add mini white candy stars or white chocolate chips.

For a summery addition to your home, fill blue canning jars and vases with red and white geraniums.

Try this refreshing Independence Day dessert: Partially fill clear parfait glasses with blueberries, or blueberry or blue raspberry sherbet. Next add vanilla ice cream, marshmallow fluff or white chocolate chips. Top with fresh strawberries or raspberries, strawberry ice cream or red sherbet.

Line a basket with a patriotic napkin and fill with star-shaped cookies decorated with red, white and blue sprinkles. Another idea: use the cookies as decorations on cakes and cupcakes.

As an alternative to fruit salad, try serving fruit kabobs. Thread strawberries, cherries and watermelon cubes alternating with a line of blueberries onto long thin flag skewers. Serve in a large bowl filled with ice. Alongside, place a small dish of whipped cream, garnished with blue sprinkles.

Key Idea

*For a festive
cooler, line a big
red wagon with
large plastic
bags and
fill with ice.*

Serve a patriotic fruit, vegetable and cheese tray. Some suggestions:

- Red: cherries, cherry tomatoes, raspberries, radishes, red apples, red peppers, red plums, straw-berries, and cold water-melon wedges.
- White: cauliflower, jicama, sour cream dip, whipped cream and white cheese cubes or slices.
- Blue: blueberries—what else?

If your party includes children, make up some fun treat bags. Decorate small cellophane bags or Chinese take-out containers (found at specialty packaging or candy shops) with flags and stars. Put in a small flag, a small box of safe fireworks, such as paper "poppers" (if age-appropriate), a small squirt gun and a pack of fizzy "exploding" candy. Pack these with red, white and blue shredded paper.

Help your kids paint a flag on their faces with face paint. If you have daughters, they can paint their fingernails and toenails with a small flag or star design.

For a unique centerpiece, try using a watermelon placed sideways. Cut a small opening out of the top that is just big enough to be able to stick your hand inside and scoop out the fruit. Carve out star, flag or firecracker designs and insert a few votive candles or one small candle (just as you would with a pumpkin). Another idea: Cut the watermelon in half and scoop out the in-sides to form a bowl. Line with plastic wrap and fill with water. Place red, white and blue floating candles and flag confetti. If you don't choose to use this bowl as a center-piece, it makes a great fruit salad bowl.

NOTES

NOTES

AUTUMN

AUTUMN TRADITIONS

Change the pictures on your refrigerator to scenes of autumn and Halloween. It's easy to get excited when you are surrounded with happy memories of family pastime activities, like visiting the pumpkin patch.

Make homemade caramel corn or caramel apples . . . or make both!

When wrapping fall gifts, use raffia or ribbons in deep autumn colors. Tuck a fall flower, such as a pansy, or a beautiful leaf into the ribbon.

Steep your home with the warm, delicious scents of autumn. Purchase scented candles and potpourri in apple-cinnamon, ginger-bread, maple or pumpkin pie fragrances.

Turn raking leaves into a fun family activity. If the kids get to play first, they may even want to help! Create leaf mazes and use a stop-watch to see who can finish first. Or set up a broad jump and see who can jump as far as the pile of leaves. Take pictures of everyone jumping into huge leafy piles. A sneaky way to end the fun is to make a contest out of who can fill the lawn bags first.

scarecrows

Make a family project out of creating a scarecrow, choose a different character design each year. One year he might be your favorite football star; the next, a lady gardener complete with watering can . . . who knows! Next, decide if you would like the scarecrow to stand in your garden or on your porch, or if it will be sitting down. This will determine the length of the stick or pole you will need to connect the head to the body. If the scarecrow is sitting down, you will need a short stick that will go from the bottom of the head to the waist; if standing, choose a long stick, that will go all the way from the head to the bottom of one leg. If you want stiff arms, you will need an additional small stick to go across the chest.

Here is a list of items and accessories to spark your imagination and give your creation "character." Many of these materials can be found around your house or purchased at a garage sale or thrift shop:

- A stick, a broom handle or a pole (or two)

- Newspaper, leaves, hay, batting or other stuffing material

- Rubber bands or twine to tie off the wrists, shirttail, and ankles

Head:

- A painted pumpkin, large gourd or squash, or one decorated with natural materials such as twigs, Indian corn, pumpkin seeds, acorns, pine cones, etc. Here's an idea: Position the pumpkin so that the top (stem) is facing the front. Now you have a funny-shaped nose. *Note:* You will need to cut a hole in the bottom of the pumpkin or gourd to connect the head to the body with your stick.

- A stuffed and decorated brown grocery bag

- An empty plastic milk jug or styrofoam wig mold covered with pantyhose or a solid colored muslin, denim, or burlap. Another alternative is to stuff the fabric with batting and tie off to form a ball. Glue on facial features cut out of fabric or use waterproof fabric markers.

- An upside-down metal bucket—paint the eyes, nose and mouth with acrylic paints. You could use a rusty bucket (or one that is spray painted to look rusty) for a "country scarecrow."

Hair:

- Wig

- Yarn or raffia (this works great for pigtails)

- Broom bristles (use the broom handle for your supporting stick and show the top of the broom with only the bristles poking through the top of the head). A mop could be used in the same way.

- Twigs for wild hair (you'll need to drill small holes first)

- Leaves or corn husks

- The stem on the pumpkin (especially great if long and curved) for a ponytail

- Curling ribbon

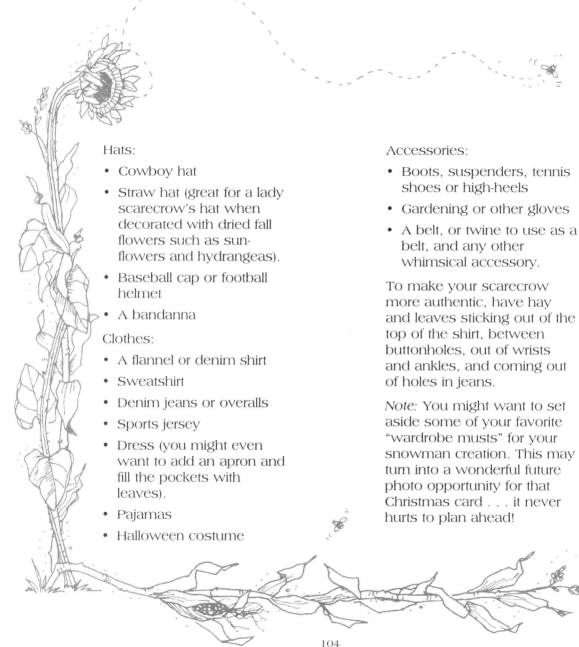

Hats:

- Cowboy hat
- Straw hat (great for a lady scarecrow's hat when decorated with dried fall flowers such as sun-flowers and hydrangeas).
- Baseball cap or football helmet
- A bandanna

Clothes:

- A flannel or denim shirt
- Sweatshirt
- Denim jeans or overalls
- Sports jersey
- Dress (you might even want to add an apron and fill the pockets with leaves).
- Pajamas
- Halloween costume

Accessories:

- Boots, suspenders, tennis shoes or high-heels
- Gardening or other gloves
- A belt, or twine to use as a belt, and any other whimsical accessory.

To make your scarecrow more authentic, have hay and leaves sticking out of the top of the shirt, between buttonholes, out of wrists and ankles, and coming out of holes in jeans.

Note: You might want to set aside some of your favorite "wardrobe musts" for your snowman creation. This may turn into a wonderful future photo opportunity for that Christmas card . . . it never hurts to plan ahead!

If you would like your scarecrow to light up on Halloween night, substitute a carved pumpkin for the existing head. Cut a small hole in the back of the pumpkin and insert a flashlight or a small string of Christmas lights.

Have your scarecrow propped up on a bale of hay, sitting in a wheelbarrow, in an old chair on your porch, or standing in the garden. Take the weather into account when deciding on the perfect place. Surround him with cornstalks and pumpkins. This wonderful guest can be displayed throughout the fall season.

Start a fun neighborhood tradition and have a scarecrow decorating contest. This would be a great theme to go along with a potluck or progressive dinner. Then let the neighbors vote. As an extra bonus, imagine how festive your street will look!

Here's another thought: Make a scarecrow and donate it to a senior center, or supply the materials for the residents to assemble one. What a wonderful way to spread autumn joy!

Key Idea

Purchase or grow sugar pumpkins and make a pumpkin pie from scratch.

~ Spend a crisp Saturday or Sunday at your local county fair. It's a wonderful way to spend the afternoon, with a little something to satisfy every member of your family. Marvel at the giant-sized produce, enjoy the animal shows and displays, eat scones, and have a good scream on the rides! Who knows. . . you might even be inclined to enter your special family jam or pie!

~ Celebrate the season by making an assortment of leaf-shaped sugar cookies. Decorate with a variety of autumn-colored frostings and sprinkles, and pipe on "veins" with brown frosting. Another idea: Make a square or rectangular gingerbread cake and cut into pieces. While still warm, place a stencil in the shape of a leaf over each piece, sprinkle with powdered sugar and remove the stencil.

~ If you have planted a pumpkin patch this summer, have some fun with it. When your pumpkins are still small, you can slide them into interestingly-shaped con-tainers—a rectangular milk carton, for example. When the pumpkin matures, it will take on the shape of the container. You will have the only "square" pumpkin on the block. What a perfect shape for a Frankenstein. If you scratch your name or a message on the pumpkin while it is still small, the letters will magically grow as the pumpkin does.

~ Create a fall atmosphere in your front yard by filling a wheelbarrow, wagon, planter, or your garden with pansies, mums, kale, and small, bright yellow sunflowers.

~ If you are mailing someone special a card or letter this time of year, tuck in an apple-cinnamon flavored tea bag or sprinkle some leaf-shaped confetti into the envelope.

Make homemade donuts. A fast and easy method: Use canned refrigerator biscuits. Cut out the middle with a liter-sized soda pop lid and deep fry in one inch of hot oil for approximately one minute or until lightly brown on both sides. When slightly cool, shake one or two at a time in a small paper bag partially filled with sugar, powdered sugar, or a mix of cinnamon and sugar.

Hold a children's sunflower growing contest (this would require pre-planning). You would need to plant the sunflowers in early summer and mark each with a waterproof marker identifying each child gardener. Give out ribbons for tallest, most unique, etc.

Try different recipes of homemade apple cider. Have a taste test to determine your official family recipe.

Bundle up, pack a thermos of hot chocolate, and enjoy a soccer or football game. Pack a tailgate picnic to enjoy at half-time.

Make dessert in the shape of a soccer ball or football. This is easy to do on cakes, cupcakes, or cookies cut with a round cookie cutter. Simply frost the item with bright colored frosting, and pipe on the soccer ball design with black. If you want a football-shaped cake, bake a rectangular cake. When it's cool, cut into a football shape. Frost with tan frosting, pipe on "stitching" with dark brown frosting, and use white for laces.

Fill clear lamp bases with candy corn, mini-pumpkins, or other small candies wrapped in harvest colored foils.

NOTES

NOTES

Back to School

Celebrate the beginning of a new school year by preparing a special (yet easy) breakfast. One year my kids wanted bacon, strawberries and donut holes!

Buy a box of magnetic words (available at stationery and gift shops) and stick them on your refrigerator or buy a small chalkboard and hang it in your kitchen. Use it to kick off the mornings with a positive message for the day.

Take a few candid photographs of your children as they are getting ready for the first day of school. Allow extra time so it won't add additional stress. One of my favorite pictures is of my daughter, complete with backpack on, looking out the window with great anticipation. You might want to take your official first day of school picture in the same location each year for continuity. If your child rides the bus, take a group picture with his or her friends at the bus stop, one as your child is getting on the bus, and then one as he is getting off the bus later that afternoon.

FOR MY TEACHER

Remember... Be the best you can be! ♡ mom

♡ If your child is starting kindergarten and is nervous about separation, here are a few suggestions to make this transition a little smoother. Give her something small of yours that she can touch if she needs comfort. I gave my daughter my small heart necklace (on which I put many kisses). She felt better those first few days wearing it. A friend of mine gave her son her small hankie that fit easily into his pocket. She also bought him a watch so he could see just what time his mom was going to be picking him up.

Personalize your child's lunch bag. Buy a variety of paper lunch bags with different designs or design your own. Purchase seasonal stickers and rubber stamps, or use markers. Have fun being creative.

Let your child plan his first day's lunch menu.

Throughout the year, put a little surprise in your child's lunch. It could be a note or a small treat. For a sweet idea, take a trip to your local specialty candy shop and see if they have something fun to include. An idea for the first day of school might be to make a small treat bag with a fall theme: Put in small candies in the shapes of apples, HERSHEY'S KISSES® chocolates in fall-colored foils and sour candies in the shapes of kids. Anything you do will be a small reminder that you were thinking about them.

♡ Hold a special celebration for good report cards. Go on a family outing to a special sporting event or other favorite destination, or have a treat at home.

112

♡ If your child has a school presentation that he is nervous about, put an encouraging note or funny joke in his notebook or lunch bag. If your younger child is "Star of the Week" in his classroom, put something "star-studded" into his lunch. You could cut his sandwich into a star shape, decorate his orange with small star stickers, or put in a small bag of star-shaped cookies.

🥣 Commemorate the first day of school with a special dinner so the children can share all their exciting news. Have a toast to the new school year with sparkling cider. Purchase a unique plate or fancy glass that your child gets to use at dinner time to celebrate achieving a goal at school or other special accomplishment.

🎁 Buy a small photo album for each of your children to keep their school photos organized. Put their favorite school picture on one side of the page and on the other side attach a small blank piece of paper with the grade your child is in written on top. Have your child sign her name and write a small message at the end of the year depicting the memorable moments of that grade. At the beginning of each school year bring it out and compare! Share pictures of yourself and your spouse as school children.

♡ Make a date to have lunch with your child during the school year. You could bring lunch from a favorite fast-food restaurant, pack a special lunch for two, or let him order for both of you from the lunch cart.

NOTES

Halloween

Call your local bakery and order orange-and-black swirled bread just in time for Halloween lunches.

For a fun classroom or home party, have each parent send in trick-or-treat items for each party guest. Suggest candy only as a last resort! Items might include Halloween pencils, erasers, stickers, stencils, bookmarks, rings, small bags of peanuts, fruit snacks, etc. If you want an additional activity, let the kids decorate their own bags. Each child goes down the line collecting their "goodies."

Add color to your porch by painting some of your pumpkins before carving. Paint a pumpkin green for a witch, or if you have a long, skinny one . . . how about a Frankenstein? Poke in Tootsie® Pops, corks, or pumpkin pieces for the neck bolts. Use white paint for a ghost or black for a cat.

Serve cheeseburgers for dinner. Cut the cheese into a jack-o-lantern face design and melt on hamburger. Serve open-faced on a plate.

Serve orange punch or pop in clear glasses and insert black straws. Or how about using a black licorice piece for a stir stick? If age-appropriate, add ice cubes containing washed black plastic spiders.

Play a memory game. The first person says, for example, "I'm going trick-or-treating and I'm going to get a pack of gum," the next person repeats the first statement and adds one thing, "I'm going trick-or-treating and I'm going to get a pack of gum and a caramel apple." If you forget to say something, you are out. The game continues until there is only one person left.

Set a photo album on the coffee table featuring all the highlights from past Halloweens. Add to it each year.

Wrap up treat bags or other goodies in small squares of black and orange netting and tie with orange or black ribbon.

Cut off the top half of a pumpkin and scoop out the insides to form a bowl (a wide, flat-sitting one works best). Cut the top edge in a zigzag pattern and line with plastic wrap. Fill with water, put in some black floating candles and Halloween confetti and you have a great centerpiece! Or fill the plastic-lined pumpkin with trick-or-treat candy, popcorn, or small gifts for party favors.

Serve nacho cheese dip with "black" (blue corn) tortilla chips.

If your child's birthday falls around Halloween, carve a pumpkin with a birthday cake or party hat design.

Remember how much fun it was to make a gingerbread house at Christmas? Repeat the experience by making a haunted house. Hold your graham cracker pieces together with piped-on black royal icing. Decorate with Halloween candies, make a graveyard with cookie crumbs, add cobwebs, spiders, skeletons, etc., and make small signs that read "Turn Back Now!", "Enter At Your Own Risk", or "Keep Out." You might have so much fun you'll want to create a whole ghost town!

For an easy and unique jack-o-lantern, use cookie cutters as stencils before carving. Just a simple design of stars and moons, for example, will shine brightly on Halloween night.

Keep your Halloween punch cold with this ghoulish addition: Fill surgical gloves (available at drug stores) with green punch and insert gummy worms or vines from grapes for "veins." Tie and freeze the glove. Unwrap and use "hand" to float in your Halloween punch bowl.

For alternatives to neighborhood trick-or-treating, check into the activities offered in your community. Many malls offer trick-or-treating, churches sometimes hold harvest festivals, and schools have Halloween carnivals. Also, look into "haunted houses," zoos, and public swimming pools that sometimes offer a "haunted swim night."

When carving your jack-o-lanterns, use an ice cream scoop to easily hollow out the insides.

🥣 Experiment with different flavorings when roasting pumpkin seeds. After cleaning seeds, put into a bowl with a small amount of oil or melted butter to coat. Add garlic, nacho cheese flavoring, parmesan cheese, cinnamon and sugar, brown sugar, Worcestershire sauce, or any other family favorite. Transfer to a cookie sheet and roast at 350 degrees for about 35 minutes, stirring every 10 minutes, or until lightly toasted.

🏠 Enjoy autumn-scented votive candles such as apple, cinnamon, and pumpkin in your jack-o-lanterns and other indoor Halloween decorations that require candles.

🥣 Make individual bags of trail mix and add candy such as candy corn or Halloween M&M's® brand chocolate candies for color. For a healthier alternative, add chopped up dried apricots and raisins. Package in cellophane bags with Halloween designs. Tie with black shoestring licorice.

🥣 For a fun party activity or favor, try this classic idea: Take a clear plastic glove (found at most bakeries) and place one candy corn, with the pointed side down, in each finger for the "finger-nails." Fill the remainder with popcorn and tie with orange and black curling ribbon. Top off with a spider ring.

🏠 Keep your house as dark as possible on Halloween night. Light candles as well as jack-o-lanterns, make a fire in the fireplace, and use Hallow-een lights and decorations to provide your atmosphere.

🥣 Make caramel apples and roll immediately in black and orange sprinkles or crushed candy corn. Or create a jack-o-lantern face using shapes cut out of fruit leather.

Older kids love word search puzzles and scrambled word games, which are fun to create with a Halloween theme.

Discover the many uses for pipe cleaners. Twist them to form black cat heads, witches hats, spiders or orange pumpkins. Use as napkin rings or as package tie-ons.

Hold a neighborhood decorating party. Have on hand an assortment of colored construction paper. Have the children cut out and decorate paper pumpkins, haunted houses, bats, spiders, and skeletons. Decorate your windows with this original artwork and treat the artists to donuts with hot spiced cider.

Connect a grouping of jack-o-lanterns with a spider web and black plastic spiders for a spookier effect.

Check with your local bakeries to see what they provide for seasonal treats. You could always go with something ready-made, but if the bakery decorates its own pastries, why not go with something different? Try, for example, a Persian donut frosted with a spider web design, complete with a spider ring. Or attach a seasonal candy or small toy to a decorated cupcake.

Use your imagination when decorating outdoors. For example, if you have a lamppost in front of a bush, place a mask over the lamppost and drape the bush with a sheet. You'll have an instant scary monster!

119

Carve a different letter on individual pumpkins to create a Halloween message.

Carve large navel oranges to look like mini jack-o-lanterns. Fill each with ice cream, frozen yogurt or sherbet, and freeze until ready to serve. Or make purple, yellow or green gelatin. When it's partially set, scoop into a carved orange and refrigerate until firm.

For a scary addition to your holiday decorations, visit your local costume and display or thrift shop. Many have large cardboard cut-outs of horror creatures. Imagine what a hit it would be to have Frankenstein, Dracula, or the witch from the *Wizard of Oz* as "guests" at your Halloween party. During the year, check your video rental store. Some horror movie posters even come with small lights, making the characters' eyes glow. Put your name in early if you see a good poster.

Older children love to have a neighborhood scavenger hunt during a Halloween party.

For an easy dessert, transform a cake, cupcakes or cookies (cut with a round cookie cutter) into one of many Halloween symbols that have a round shape. For example, you could decorate a cake or serve a tray of "eyeballs" or jack-o-lantern cookies or cupcakes. How about turning a dark choco-late frosted cupcake into a Halloween cat? Put two HERSHEY'S KISSES® chocolates on top for ears. Pipe on white frosting whiskers and a face. Use small round candies for eyes.

Carve or decorate gourds as well as pumpkins. Small white ones make great mini ghosts and green ones make wonderful witches.

Play a story game by filling a plastic pumpkin with small items such as a piece of candy, an eye patch, a small flashlight, and any other fun or ghoulish item you can find. Set the scene by starting the story, then have each child pull out an item on their turn and use the item to continue the story for a pre-determined period of time.

If you would like to limit your child's candy intake, but still keep the trick-or-treat fun, consider this alternative. Let your child keep twenty pieces of candy and pay him a nickel for each piece that gets thrown away.

Have hot cider, roasted pumpkin seeds, and a basket full of flavored popcorn waiting for your cold trick-or-treaters when they return (see page 118 for roasted pumpkin seeds recipe).

Serve orange sherbet mixed with mini chocolate chips. Put a scoop into Halloween cupcake liners or freeze between dark chocolate cookies to make ice cream sandwiches.

Create a Halloween tree. Spray bare tree branches black and plant them in a terra cotta pot or in a brown paper bag weighed down with small rocks. Tie with orange and black raffia or a seasonal ribbon. String the branches with tiny lights and tie on frosted Halloween cookies (poke a hole with a small straw before baking) or ornaments. Add to the tree each year.

Decorate a spooky cake by creating a ghost made with stiff royal icing. Position him to look like he is coming out of the top with the tail coming out the side at the bottom. This will give the illusion of the ghost going through the cake.

Make popcorn ball jack-o-lanterns by tinting the popcorn orange before shaping into balls. Pipe on frosting or use candy corn for faces. A green gumdrop makes a wonderful stem.

If you are planning a party, make your own invitations instead of buying them. Use the back of paper masquerade masks, cut out a paper black bat with fold-out wings, or make a scroll and insert into a skull or spider ring. Another classic idea is to write your invitation on the back of a white handkerchief or napkin. Wrap around a Tootsie® Pop, tie with a ribbon and draw on a face.

Dip halves of dried apricots in dark chocolate and let dry. Wrap in decorated cellophane bags for gifts.

Serve a pudding or custard with a whipped cream ghost on the top. Complete the ghost with round sprinkles for eyes.

Line your walkways with luminaries. Decorate paper lunch bags by drawing on a message traced with a stencil. Write a friendly or scary message or a word on each bag; for example: "WELCOME, TRICK OR TREATERS," and "HAVE FUN." Or a spooky message: "ENTER AT YOUR OWN RISK —BEWARE!" Have an adult cut out the letters with a craft knife. Fill the bottom of each bag with sand (approximately one to two inches) and place a votive or tea candle inside. You could also use tin coffee cans painted orange like jack-o-lanterns, outline the design with nail holes.

Host a neighborhood pumpkin carving night. Give out ribbons for funniest, scariest and most unique. Line up your jack-o-lanterns, illuminate them, and take an annual picture. Have the previous years' pictures on display so you can outdo yourselves each year!

Encourage your kids to decorate their rooms. They can turn their rooms into a haunted house by stringing cobwebs and lights. If you have young children, supply the materials for them to make costumes for their stuffed animals and dolls. It's easy to cut out a ghost costume from white fabric. Make a mummy by wrapping with gauze. You could even get more elaborate by pulling out the sewing machine!

Make spider cupcakes. Frost cupcakes with white frosting. Pipe on circles of black icing with the largest on the outside to the smallest in the middle. Pull your knife down from the center towards the outside to form the web. In the middle of each, put a spider created with frosting, or make one by using a black gumdrop with black shoestring licorice legs.

Dip small pretzels in white chocolate and let dry. Drizzle the pretzels with thinned orange and black frosting. When set, wrap up in a cellophane bag and tie with raffia or a Halloween ribbon. This makes a nice teacher's or hostess' gift.

Act crazy and surprise the kids by cooking breakfast in Halloween attire. It could be as simple as painted scars on your face or fake fur stuck onto the back of your hands. Try to act serious and see how long it takes them to notice!

Make "witch's brew." Fill small lidded jars with spices, food items, candies, etc. that resemble body parts; peeled grapes for eyes, little pieces of white netting for flies' wings, cut off white tips from candy corn for cats' teeth, etc. and put on labels. Put these around a punch bowl (a large black pot would be great) filled with cider and don't forget the dry ice.

Play a game of GHOST bingo, using candy corn game pieces or "Hang Frankenstein" (Hangman), complete with neck bolts and jagged-edged pants.

Serve a plate of "eyeball" or jack-o-lantern bagels for lunch. For eyeballs: Spread mini bagels with cream cheese and put a black olive or cherry tomato in the center. Pipe on red-tinted cream cheese (slightly thinned with milk) or use thin wavy strips of red peppers for the "blood-shot" part. For jack-o-lanterns: Spread the bagels with orange-tinted cream cheese. Use yellow or green peppers for the jack-o-lantern features and serve open-faced.

Fill small clear bags with orange and black jelly beans or seasonal M&M's® brand chocolate candies. Tie with curling Halloween ribbon or raffia. Give these to special friends who come to your home to trick-or-treat.

NOTES

NOTES

NOTES

The day after Halloween (or shortly thereafter), set out a small box or a small basket of paper scraps. Each time a family member feels thankful for something or someone, have them fill out a piece of paper and put it into the box. Be sure to include an equal number of compliments for everyone who will be attending your Thanksgiving dinner. Right before dessert, read the notes. You will be surprised at the amount of things we are all grateful for, yet rarely express. Here's a variation: Have a basket of small magnets also available, and each time someone fills out a small note, have them attach the note to your refrigerator. This way you can be reminded all month.

Have a table set up with a big jigsaw puzzle to provide an alternative activity while dinner is cooking.

Have each guest at your Thanksgiving dinner bring a gift for a worthy cause. Donate a non-perishable food item to a local food bank or an item for a needy family basket or toy drive.

After everyone has had a chance to rest from the Thanksgiving feast, bring out one last surprise. Set a tray in the center of your table with coffee and hot chocolate garnishes. Hollow out mini pumpkins and line with plastic wrap. Fill each with a different flavoring such as whipped cream, sugar cubes, cinnamon sticks, chocolate sticks or chocolate-dipped spoons. You could even line the tray with beautiful fall leaves.

♡ Invite someone to your Thanksgiving dinner who would otherwise be alone.

🥣 Have a special family breakfast while watching the Thanksgiving Day Parade on TV. If you have young children, make Indian or tepee pancakes. For an Indian face: Tuck three bacon strips behind the pancake for the "feathered headdress." Provide squeeze bottles of maple and berry-flavored syrups to decorate the face and headdress. For tepees: Fold under two edges of a large pancake to form a triangular shape. Position bacon underneath to look like it is sticking out of the top of the tepee. Decorate with flavored syrups.

🥄 Start a family tradition out of taking a long walk after dinner (weather permitting).

🏠 Decorate your table with harvest accessories. Serve dips for crackers and vegetables in hollowed out mini pumpkins, small cabbages, or orange peppers. Illuminate your table by hollowing out apples to form a shallow well (sprinkle with lemon juice to preserve color). Insert a votive candle or small tea light and place one by each place setting.

🎁 For a special gift for a teacher, hostess or dinner guest, consider this easy idea: Make fudge or jelly bean-filled cookie cutters. Buy cookie cutters in the shapes of leaves, pumpkins, or turkeys. For fudge: Place cutters on a parchment paper-lined cookie sheet. Make maple fudge and pour into cutters. When set, wrap each in cellophane and tie with raffia. For jelly beans: Pack each tightly with gourmet autumn-colored jelly beans and wrap.

🐦 For a fun children's activity, as well as a delicious snack, create edible apple turkeys. Each child will need an apple, toothpicks and an assortment of edible decorations. Here are a few ideas:

- large and small marshmallows
- raisins
- dried cherries or other dried fruit
- gumdrops
- licorice pieces
- cloves

Have the kids place their apples sideways and attach a large marshmallow with a toothpick for the head. Cloves make great eyes. Poke in two toothpicks for the legs and several in the back to create a fanned-out tail. Embellish the toothpicks with a variety of candy and dried fruit. Set one by each artist's place setting at dinner.

Caution: Because toothpicks are sharp, this would not be appropriate for very young children without supervision.

You might want to make up the turkeys in advance with only the apples and toothpicks. Break off the sharp points of the exposed ends. Tell the kids to slide off the decorations to eat. Then let an adult remove the toothpicks before eating apples.

♡ Send a card or postcard thanking those special people who have made a difference in your life or in the life of someone you love.

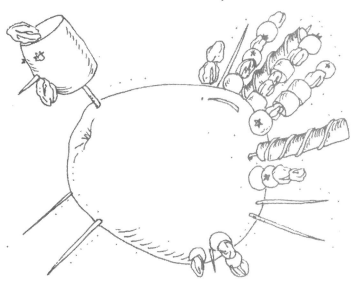

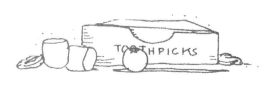

NOTES

NOTES

CHILDHOOD TRADITIONS

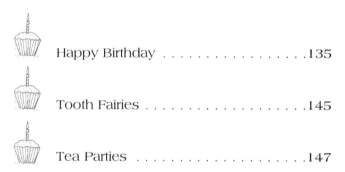

HAPPY BIRTHDAY

For Baby's first birthday, buy a keepsake gift. You might purchase a brightly decorated cake plate and write the child's name and birth date on the back. Or buy a special vase and write the child's name and date on the bottom. Each year on your child's birthday fill with his or her favorite flowers. When buying birthday cake candle holders, look around for something unique—for example, a miniature silver train candle holder set with an engine and six cars. On baby's first birthday, use just the engine. Each year you would add another car until the child turned six, when the entire set would be on top of the cake. Any one of these gifts would make a wonderful heirloom!

Make cake "ice cream cones." Put old-fashioned ice cream cones into muffin tins and wrap foil around each base to hold them in place. Fill each three-fourths full of cake batter. Bake according to cupcake time. When cooled, swirl in whipped cream, or pipe on frosting to look like "soft serve" ice cream and decorate.

Sneak into your child's room the night before his birthday and decorate with streamers and balloons, or just fill the bedroom closet with balloons. Put a small present at the foot of your child's bed so he wakes up to a surprise, or tuck one into his backpack.

For preteens or teenagers arrange a scavenger hunt at their favorite hangout . . . the mall!

You would be surprised at the many free items the stores give away. You can get balloons, product samples, candy, movie pins, mini shopping bags, bookmarks, postcards, etc.

Have the party guests form two teams, and provide a list of clues for each. Each team goes into the stores listed on the clue sheet in order, and either writes down an answer or picks up a free product. The list might include, for example, "Write down the names of six villains on display at the Disney Store" or "Find the price on the Ken Griffey Jr. autographed baseball at The Locker Room." Have each team work in opposite directions and have a designated spot located in the center of the mall to be the finish line. The first team to complete the list and get there first wins!

Bake a three-layer birthday cake with each layer being a different flavor.

Enroll the birthday child in your "special book club." Make a gift certificate and tuck it into the birthday card. Send books throughout the year in the mail. This surprise would be enjoyed by kids of all ages and would make a great gift from grandparents or out-of-town relatives and friends.

For a fast alternative to scooping ice cream at a party, put individual scoops of ice cream in paper cupcake liners ahead of time. Decorate and freeze until needed.

If your older child's birthday falls during the school year, have flowers, or a balloon, candy or cookie bouquet delivered to her at school.

Decorate your breakfast table in full birthday style, down to putting a candle in your child's pancakes (or whatever is his or her favorite breakfast).

For parties on the go, here are a few possibilities.

Artistic:
- Hands-on pottery shop
- Recording studio to record a song
- Rubber stamp lesson

Entertainment:
- Amusement park
- Children's museum
- Magic show
- Play or musical performance
- Puppet show
- Remote control car track
- Science center

Outdoors:
- Beach for sand castle building contest or volleyball game
- Camping
- Canoeing or kayaking
- Hiking
- Kite flying

Sports:
- Baseball game or batting cage
- Basketball
- Bowling
- Dance class
- Go-carts
- Gymnastics
- Horseback riding
- Ice skating
- Indoor facility for mountain climbing
- Karate or other martial arts lesson
- Putt-Putt golf
- Racquetball
- Roller skating or roller blading
- Skateboarding
- Skiing or inner tubing
- Sporting event
- Swimming
- Tennis

Something different:
- Aquarium
- Astrology, fortune teller or palm reader (check out ahead of time and make sure they will only make fun and upbeat predictions).
- Beauty school for hairstyles, makeovers or manicures
- Farm
- Fire station
- Hot tub
- Rent a hotel suite
- Rent a limousine
- Take a short train ride
- Zoo

Decorate your front door to announce your child's birthday party, or make a sign and post it with an arrow pointing to the front door. It could read "The party is here!" "Look who's 8!" or make it theme appropriate; if you are having a slumber party, "Allison's Bed and Breakfast" or an art party, "Marissa's Art Gallery."

Plan your child's birthday theme together months in advance. That way, you can pick up favors and decorations as you see them, and everyone can share the anticipation of the big day.

If you would like an entertainer to perform at your home, look at the ideas on the previous page, or check in the entertainment section of your phone book.

Use your imagination when coming up with birthday themes. Your library or bookstore has a good selection to get you motivated. Take time to brainstorm with your child to come up with original party ideas.

One year my daughter wanted a "Price Is Right" birthday party for her 12th birthday. From watching the TV show, we got a lot of ideas for fun games and props. We made giant name tags and hung a big sign behind the couch that read "CONTESTANT'S ROW." This was a fun party where our good friends also got involved. We had a game show host, announcers and merchandise models. The kids earned a turn to play one of the games by guessing the retail price of a product. Some of the games included "Hole In One," "Secret X," and "In the Bag," just like the show. Everyone got a turn and everyone won (with the help of the other contestants). A prize table was set up with assorted wrapped gifts and the winners chose their prizes. We even had "The Showcase" where everyone had a chance to win the "big prize." Does your child have a favorite game show?

When decorating for a birthday party, look around your home for instant decorating ideas. For example, if giving a sports theme party, line a football helmet or a baseball glove with a cloth napkin and fill with snacks. What about covering a bright, solid colored tablecloth with black netting to look like a soccer goal? Fill water bottles with candies and other small party gifts.

Be creative when coming up with ideas for treat bags. Kids will appreciate anything, but if you are looking for something unique, here are a few suggestions:

- Take a small colored paper bag and fold the top over a few times. Make two holes in the middle of the fold with a paper punch, weave a colorful ribbon through the holes, and tie.

- Cut squares from two colors of fabric netting (available at fabric stores). Put your treats in the center, gather up the corners and tie with curling ribbon or star garland.

- Wrap up small gifts and treats in a bandanna and tie with a thin rope or raffia.

- Jazz up a small plastic zip-lock bag with markers or stickers. Or use a decorated, clear cello-phane bag and tie with bright shoelaces or a licorice shoestring.

Have the "goodie" bags personalized in advance or let the kids personalize their own party favor at the birthday party. Try, for example: Small plastic boxes or pencil cups, clear cosmetic bags, small flowerpots, sun visors, baseball hats, sporting goods, or even white pillowcases.

If you are decorating something plastic, use paint pens (available at craft stores), or for fabric items, use fabric paints.

When wrapping a birthday gift for a first birthday, tuck one candle in the ribbon before tying the bow.

If your child's birthday falls on a school day, surprise him at school with lunch from a favorite restaurant, or let him design a special menu for his sack lunch. Decorate the bag with stickers or rubber stamps.

Bring out pictures and videos of the birthday child as a baby and of early birthday parties.

For a great birthday party surprise, rent a cotton candy maker. Call your local party supply rental store for other unique ideas.

Serve the birthday child's meals on a special plate that is used only for birthdays, accomplishments and special times.

For a fun party decoration and favor, put a clear pitcher or vase of multi-colored twisted straws in the center of your party table.

As an alternative to birthday cake, make decorated ice cream sandwiches. Make the birthday child's favorite cookies and cut out a shape with a cookie cutter. Decorate with sprinkles or small candies. Poke a hole in the middle of the birthday child's cookie with a birthday candle before baking (now he can still insert a candle and make a birthday wish). When cooled, sandwich ice cream between two cookies and freeze until serving.

One custom is to put an extra candle on the birthday cake "to grow on." This will symbolize the year to come.

Decorate your birthday plates before serving dessert. Sift powdered sugar onto plates and sprinkle with colored crystallized sugar for a confetti look.

Modify the classic game of "Pin the Tail on the Donkey" to fit any party theme. At my daughter's friend's birthday party, the kids stuck cut out paper "kisses" on a poster of a teen idol!

Make a tray of decorated birthday cupcakes and top each with a cookie to go along with your theme. Or arrange a platter of frosted cupcakes that spell out HAPPY BIRTHDAY! Another decoration: Sprinkle colored coconut on frosted cupcakes. Put the coconut on while the frosting is still soft and use colors that coordinate with your party. Place a small party favor on top of each.

For a great thank you note, give your guests a photograph of themselves having fun at the party. Have your child write her note on the back. Or give each guest a mini collage of pictures and a thank you note, all in one. Take several pictures of everyone having a fun time, mount them on paper, make copies and have your child write her note on the front.

Make a giant birthday cookie. Use your child's favorite cookie recipe and make one giant cookie on a pizza pan or cookie sheet. Pipe on a birthday message with frosting.

Write each child's name on a balloon. Tie a balloon onto the back of each chair and you have an instant party seating arrangement. Decorate the birthday child's chair with several balloons and bright ribbon streamers. Include a mylar birthday balloon or a balloon to fit your theme.

A guaranteed hit for a birthday party is to set up an ice cream sundae bar. Toppings might include hot fudge, caramel sauce, fruit, cut up candy bars, cookie crumbs, favorite small candies, cut up brownies, or any other favorites. Don't forget the cherries and a can of whipped cream—there's something about squirting that can that's irresistible! A milkshake bar is also a great idea. Have a good variety of ice cream flavors, syrups and candies by your blender and let each make their own special concoction.

If your child would like a slumber party away from home, there are many possibilities that are only a phone call away. Did you know that many museums, zoos, aquariums, science centers, athletic clubs, as well as recreation centers offer sleep-overs?

Put together a birthday photo album for each child. Include the birthday party invitation, napkin, any memorabilia and, of course, lots of photographs.

Have a clear piece of plexiglass cut to fit your party table. Put on a colorful tablecloth, throw on confetti and any other theme-related decoration (sports cards, movie memorabilia, photos of the birthday child, HAPPY BIRTHDAY letters, etc.) then put on the plexiglass. This will hold down your decorations and keep everything "frosting and crumb-free." You can use this again for any holiday or other party.

Buy the year-end copy of *Life* magazine on the year your child is born. Give this later at a milestone birthday, like 16 or 21.

NOTES

Tooth fairies

♡ Listed below are a few actual accounts from children, which have led to the belief that there must be several generous tooth fairies in service!

One tooth fairy left . . .

- A trail of stardust (which looked like glow-in-the-dark glitter mixed with tiny star confetti) from the child's windowsill to her pillow.

- A trail of gold stars, moons, and pumpkins for a tooth lost on Halloween night. A few dollars were held together with a spider ring.

- For the loss of a first tooth, a starry trail from the window-sill to the bedside table that led to a book on tooth fairies. Inside the book there was a message: "Your tooth looks super! Happy Brushing! Love, The Tooth Fairy," which was written in gold glittery writing.

- Disney dollars held together with a Tinkerbell pin for a tooth lost while on vacation in Disneyland.

- A small surprise package containing a few dollars. Each time it was wrapped a little differently—one time it was in a velvety pouch; another, a small decorated keepsake box.

♡ If your child has a wiggly tooth that is really ready, have them bite into a nice soft banana. It really works!

♡ When your child has his first loose tooth, sit down and read a story. A couple of good ones are *Little Rabbit's Loose Tooth* by Lucy Bate and *Tooth Fairy* by Audrey Wood.

NOTES

Tea Parties

♡ Take the opportunity to sit down and have tea with your kids. It is the perfect way to really talk and for them to have your undivided attention. Have a tea party to celebrate an accomplishment or special occasion. Or secretly set the table in full tea party style for breakfast, an after-school surprise, or anytime at all.

If you have younger children or grandchildren, purchase a trunk and fill it with dress-up clothes. Your local fabric store would have many ideas on how to make simple or elaborate outfits. You can also find really great items at garage sales or thrift shops as well as costume and children's clothing stores. Have a variety of hats, gloves, jewelry, dresses, and feather boas. Don't forget some hats, coats and ties for the boys!

Choose a caffeine-free tea. Some favorite flavors are: fruit, peppermint, cinnamon, almond or licorice. If your children don't care for tea, try juice, hot chocolate, pink-tinted milk or chocolate milk, cold or warm pink lemonade, hot spiced cider, punch, pink pop or any other favorite beverage.

Have a cookie tea party. Just before your tea party, try a new cookie recipe together. Then enjoy the warm cookies right out of the oven. For a special gift and keepsake, give each child a special blank cookbook or journal. After each tea party, write down the recipe, along with the date and a small memory about the day.

What do you serve at a tea party? Here are a few ideas.

Tea sandwiches and other possibilities:

- Trim off the crusts from bread and cut into small triangles, squares or cookie cutter shapes. Try pinwheels: Place a slice of bread between two pieces of waxed paper and flatten with a rolling pin. Peel away the paper, spread the bread with filling, roll up and slice into rounds.
- Order pink-tinted bread from the bakery. Sandwich fillings can be anything from the traditional cream cheese and cucumber to peanut butter and jelly.
- Mini quiches
- Cocktail franks, mini bagel pizzas, or any other favorite bite-size appetizer

Sweet treats:

- Cookies
- Cupcakes, small tea cakes, muffins, or petits fours (made or purchased)
- Scones, small tarts, or biscuits cut into a heart shape and filled with jam
- Fresh fruit or even strawberries dipped in chocolate

One way to create a lasting memory is to associate a theme with your tea parties. My Aunt Carol always gave the best tea parties for my daughter and my niece. She would use her Peter Rabbit tea set with matching dishes and accessories. These were placed on a beautiful white cutwork tablecloth. In addition, the table was decorated with china Peter Rabbit figurines.

For a springtime tea, take advantage of the beauty of primroses, pansies and other delicate flowers. Set your tea table with small clear plates. Place a small doily and/or spring flowers (that can be pressed) between two of the clear plates. Stack a set of two at each place setting. For anytime of the year, place small vases at each setting with mini bouquets.

A tea party offers a wonderful opportunity to have fun while practicing manners. Teach your kids how to have a proper English tea. You would traditionally ask, "Would you like milk or sugar?" If they would like milk, that would go into the cup first. Then, if they would like sugar, ask, "One lump or two?" Next, goes the sugar and finally the tea. Take turns serving and try to pour slowly and carefully.

Decorate cupcakes and tea cakes extra special just for tea. After frosting, sprinkle with edible glitter and/or candied flowers (page 45).

When setting your tea table, bring out all your fanciest things. Put on a lace or other elegant tablecloth, bring out your finest teapot, dishes, silver, candle holders, vases, and any other special items that don't get used nearly often enough.

Buy each of your kids a special teaspoon or teacup. Try to choose one that fits their personalities, and explain to them why you chose it. Or have a variety of cups and spoons on hand to choose from. At garage sales, thrift shops and antique stores, look for baby spoons or teaspoons, as well as other tea party "musts," such as small sugar bowls, creamers, pitchers, small trays, teacups, or elegant table linens.

Bring your tea party outside. On a sunny summer day, set your table in a nice shady spot and have a "secret garden" tea party. First, see what you have in your yard. A tree stump or a big terra cotta pot with a temporary lid makes a great table when adorned with a pretty tablecloth. Bring out all your finery and enjoy the moment.

NOTES

MARALLY PUBLISHING
Suite B
P.O. Box 1426
Mukilteo, WA 98275

❑ Please send me__ copies of your book at $14.95 per copy, plus $2.00 each to cover shipping and handling. (Washington state residents add 8.6% sales tax.)

Quantity	Item / Price	Total Price
	MEMORIES IN MOMENTS @ $14.95	
	Add $2.00 per book shipping and handling	
	Merchandise Total	
	Washington state residents add 8.6% sales tax	
	TOTAL	

❑ I don't want to order at this time, but would like to be on your mailing list for information on future publications and catalogs.

Name

Address   Apt./Suite

City   State   ZIP

Phone   (   )

Enclosed is   ❑ Check   ❑ Money Order

Credit Card   ❑ VISA   ❑ Mastercard   Exp. date

Card No.

Signature

For quick service on credit card orders,
call toll-free 1-877-MARALLY (627-2559).
If you do not want to tear this form out of the book, please feel free to photocopy it.
Or send or fax the required information on a plain sheet of paper to:
MARALLY PUBLISHING, Suite B, P.O. Box 1426, Mukilteo, WA 98275
Fax: (425) 349-5113